# History of Africa, Australia, New Zealand, Etc.

# LIBRARY OF CONGRESS CLASSIFICATION SCHEDULES

For sale by the Cataloging Distribution Service,
Library of Congress, Washington, D.C. 20541,
to which inquiries on current availability and
price should be addressed.

| | |
|---|---|
| A | General Works |
| B-BJ | Philosophy. Psychology |
| BL, BM, BP, BQ | Religion: Religions, Hinduism, Judaism, Islam, Buddhism |
| BR-BV | Religion: Christianity, Bible |
| BX | Religion: Christian Denominations |
| C | Auxiliary Sciences of History |
| D | History: General and Old World (Eastern Hemisphere) |
| DJK-DK | History of Eastern Europe (General), Soviet Union, Poland |
| DS | History of Asia |
| DT-DX | History of Africa, Australia, New Zealand, etc. |
| E-F | History: America (Western Hemisphere) |
| G | Geography. Maps. Anthropology. Recreation |
| H-HJ | Social Sciences: Economics |
| HM-HX | Social Sciences: Sociology |
| J | Political Science |
| K | Law (General) |
| KD | Law of the United Kingdom and Ireland |
| KDZ, KG-KH | Law of the Americas, Latin America and the West Indies |
| KE | Law of Canada |
| KF | Law of the United States |
| KJV-KJW | Law of France |
| KK-KKC | Law of Germany |
| L | Education |
| M | Music |
| N | Fine Arts |
| P-PA | General Philology and Linguistics Classical Languages and Literatures |
| PA Supplement | Byzantine and Modern Greek Literature Medieval and Modern Latin Literature |
| PB-PH | Modern European Languages |
| PG | Russian Literature |
| PJ-PK | Oriental Philology and Literature, Indo-Iranian Philology and Literature |
| PL-PM | Languages of Eastern Asia, Africa, Oceania; Hyperborean, Indian, and Artificial Languages |
| P-PM Supplement | Index to Languages and Dialects |
| PN, PR, PS, PZ | General Literature. English and American Literature. Fiction in English. Juvenile belles lettres |
| PQ, Part 1 | French Literature |
| PQ, Part 2 | Italian, Spanish, and Portuguese Literatures |
| PT, Part 1 | German Literature |
| PT, Part 2 | Dutch and Scandinavian Literatures |
| P-PZ | Language and Literature Tables |
| Q | Science |
| R | Medicine |
| S | Agriculture |
| T | Technology |
| U | Military Science |
| V | Naval Science |
| Z | Bibliography. Library Science |

SUBJECT CATALOGING DIVISION
PROCESSING SERVICES
LIBRARY OF CONGRESS

CLASSIFICATION

CLASS D
SUBCLASSES DT-DX

# History of Africa, Australia, New Zealand, Etc.

THIRD EDITION
LIBRARY OF CONGRESS
WASHINGTON 1989

The additions and changes in Class D, Subclasses DT–DX,
adopted while this work was in press will be cumulated and
printed in List 237 of
*LC Classification—Additions and Changes*


**Library of Congress Cataloging-in-Publication Data**

Library of Congress. Subject Cataloging Division.
    Classification. Class D, Subclasses DT–DX, history of
Africa, Australia, New Zealand, etc.
ISBN 0-8444-0649-X
    1. Classification, Library of Congress.  2. Classification—Books—History.
3. Classification—Books—Africa.  4. Classification—Books—Australia.
5. Classification—Books—New Zealand.      I. Title.
Z696.U5D 1989                    025.4'69                    89-600140
ISBN 0-8444-0649-X

For sale by the Cataloging Distribution Service,
Library of Congress, Washington, D.C. 20541
(202) 707-6100

# PREFACE

The class numbers for history were first drafted in 1901 and were later revised and published in 1916. Two supplements were published: European War (1921, 2d edition, 1933, reprinted 1954 with additions and changes) and Second World War (1947). The second edition was published in 1959, containing additions and changes incorporated in the schedules though June 1957. A reprint edition was published in 1966, containing a supplementary section of additions and changes to July 1965 that had been adopted since publication of the second edition.

The growth in size of the D schedule has necessitated the publication of the third edition in separate parts, of which DT-DX is the third to appear, following DJK-DK and DS.

As Richard S. Angell, Chief of the Subject Cataloging Division, explained in the introduction to the second edition,

> The problems of accommodating a classification schedule to change are perhaps nowhere more acute than in the field of history in this century. To account in the schedules for every change in hegemony and political alignment would initiate an amount of reclassification in this and other libraries that would have questionable economic justification. To account for none of them, however, would perpetuate some intolerable anomalies. The Library's policy has been to seek a middle ground between these two extremes. This has resulted in the retention of some of the groupings of the early 20th century, but it is believed that most of these retain a geographical justification.

The history of African countries from colonial status to independence has required many changes in the schedules. Presented for the first time in this volume are substantial changes to class numbers for Southern Africa. In order to arrange countries logically it was decided to abandon the span of numbers from DT727 to DT971 and to replace them with the span DT1001 through DT3415. This change is shown for the first time in this edition.

When Kay Elsasser, now section head of Humanities II section, was the subject cataloger responsible for Africa she developed the DT1001-DT3145 section. Nancy Jones, assistant editor of classification, completed the cumulation, updating some terminology, arranging notes and references to conform to current practice, and deleting parenthesized numbers. She also created the index and input the entire text. The responsibility for the development of the numbers themselves remains that of the subject catalogers in the Subject Cataloging Division who work in the subject areas encompassed by the schedule.

Mary K. D. Pietris
Chief, Subject Cataloging Division

Henriette D. Avram
Assistant Librarian for Processing Services

April 1989

iii

## SYNOPSIS

DT    Africa

DU    Oceania (South Seas)

DX    Gypsies

# OUTLINE

OUTLINE

DT

Africa
West Africa. West Coast - Continued

| | |
|---|---|
| 521-555.9 | French West Africa. French Sahara. West Sahara. Sahel |
| 541-541.9 | Benin. Dahomey |
| 541.42-.45 | Ethnography |
| 541.5-.845 | History |
| 541.9 | Local history and description |
| 543-543.9 | Guinea |
| 543.42-.45 | Ethnography |
| 543.5-.827 | History |
| 543.9 | Local history and description |
| 545-545.9 | Ivory Coast |
| 545.42-.45 | Ethnography |
| 545.52-.83 | History |
| 545.9 | Local history and description |
| 546.1-.49 | French-speaking Equatorial Africa |
| 546.1-.19 | Gabon (Gaboon, Gabun) |
| 546.142-.145 | Ethnography |
| 546.15-.183 | History |
| 546.19 | Local history and description |
| 546.2-.29 | Congo (Brazaville). Middle Congo |
| 546.242-.245 | Ethnography |
| 546.25-.283 | History |
| 546.29 | Local history and description |
| 546.3-.39 | Central African Republic. Central African Empire. Ubangi-Shari |
| 546.342-.345 | Ethnography |
| 546.348-.384 | History |
| 546.39 | Local history and description |
| 546.4-.49 | Chad (Tchad) |
| 546.442-.445 | Ethnography |
| 546.457-.483 | History |
| 546.49 | Local history and description |
| 547-547.9 | Niger |
| 547.42-.45 | Ethnography |
| 547.5-.83 | History |
| 547.9 | Local history and description |
| 548 | West Sahara |
| 549-549.9 | Senegal |
| 549.42-.45 | Ethnography |
| 549.47-.83 | History |
| 549.9 | Local history and description |
| 551-551.9 | Mali. Mali Federation. Soudanese Republic. French Sudan |
| 551.42-.45 | Ethnography |
| 551.5-.82 | History |
| 551.9 | Local history and description |
| 554-554.9 | Mauritania |
| 554.42-.45 | Ethnography |
| 554.52-.83 | History |
| 554.9 | Local history and description |

DT

# OUTLINE

| | |
|---|---|
| 1 | Periodicals.  Societies.  Sources and documents. |
| | Serials |
| .5 | Congresses.  Conferences, etc. |
| 2 | Gazetteers.  Guidebooks  *Dictionaries* |
| .5 | Directories |
| 3 | General works.  History of exploration |
| | Cf. G220+, History of discoveries, explorations, |
| | and travel |
| 4 | General special |
| .5 | Views |
| 5 | Compends |
| 6 | Pamphlets |
| .5 | Addresses, essays, lectures |
| | Description and travel |
| | For North Africa, <u>see</u> DT160+ |
| | For Central Sub-Saharan Africa, <u>see</u> DT348+ |
| | For East Africa, <u>see</u> DT365+ |
| | For West Africa, <u>see</u> DT470+ |
| | For South Africa, <u>see</u> DT1001+ |
| 7 | Through 1700 |
| | Cf. DT24, Africa as known to the ancients |
| 8 | 1701-1800 |
| 11 | 1801-1900 |
| 12 | 1901-1950 |
| .2 | 1951-1977 |
| .25 | 1978- |
| 13 | Antiquities |
| 14 | Social life and customs.  Civilization.  Intellectual |
| | life |
| | Ethnography |
| | Cf. GN643+, Anthropology |
| 15 | General works |
| 16 | Individual elements in the population not limited to |
| | specific territorial divisions, A-Z |

|  |  |
|---|---|
| .B2 | Bantus |
| .C48 | Chinese |
| .E17 | East Indians |
| .E95 | Europeans |
| .P8 | Pygmies |
| .S35 | Scots |
| .W45 | Whites |

**History**
17          Dictionaries.  Chronological tables, outlines, etc.
18          Biography (Collective)
            Historiography
19              General works
                Biography of historians, area studies specialists,
                    archaeologists, etc.
  .5                Collective
  .7                Individual, A-Z
            Study and teaching
                Class catalogs of audiovisual materials in .Z9A-Z
  .8                General works
  .9                By region or country, A-Z
  .95               Individual schools, A-Z
20          General works
21          General special
  .5        Military history
22          Juvenile works


**By period**
24          Africa as known to the ancients.  History and
                description
                    Cf. DT50, Egypt
                        DT168+, Carthage, etc.
25              Early through 1500
26              1501-1700
27              1701-1800
28              1801-1884
29              1884-1945
                1945-1960
30                  General works
  .2                Addresses, essays, lectures
  .5              1960-


            Political and diplomatic history.  Partition.
                Colonies and possessions
31              General works
                By period, <u>see</u> the specific period
                Relations with individual countries
                    Under each:
                        .0  Comprehensive description and history
                        .1  General special
                        .3  Early history through 1800
                        .5  1801-1960
                        .7  1960-
32              England.  Great Britain
33              France
34              Germany
35              Italy

**History**
   Political and diplomatic history.  Partition.
      Colonies and possessions
     Relations with individual countries - Continued

| | |
|---|---|
| 36 | Portugal |
| 37 | Spain |
| |    Cf. DT315.5, Moroccan question |
| |       DT653.5, Congo question |
| 38 | United States |
| .9 | Other regions or countries, A-Z |
| |    e. g.  .S65  Soviet Union |
| 39 | Red Sea coast.  Red Sea region |
| |    Including Asian portion of the Red Sea region |
| |    Cf. DT367, Northeast Africa |

**EGYPT**

| | |
|---|---|
| 43 | Periodicals.  Societies.  Sources and documents.  Serials |
| 44 | Directories |
| 45 | Guidebooks.  Gazetteers.  Dictionaries.  Directories, etc. |
| |    Including Upper and Lower Egypt |
| 46 | General works |
| 47 | Monuments and picturesque |
| 48 | General special |
| 49 | Juvenile works |
| .9 | Historical geography |
| | Description and travel |
| .98 | History of travels |
| 50 | Ancient through 637 |
| 51 | 638-1797 |
| 53 | 1798-1848 |
| 54 | 1849-1900 |
| 55 | 1901-1950 |
| 56 | 1951- |

   **Antiquities**

| | |
|---|---|
| .8 | Periodicals.  Societies.  Serials |
| .9 | General works |
| | **By period** |
| |   Ancient Egypt.  **Egyptology** |
| |     Cf. PJ1051+, History of Egyptology |
| 57 | Periodicals.  Societies.  Serials |
| |    e. g. Egypt exploration fund |

Egypt
   Antiquities
      By period
         Ancient Egypt.   Egyptology - Continued

| | |
|---|---|
| 57.5 | Private collections |
| 58 | Dictionaries |
| | Museums, exhibitions, etc. |
| .9 | General works |
| 59 | Individual.  By place, A-Z |

                e. g.   .P2  Paris.  Musée National du
                                   Louvre

| | |
|---|---|
| 60 | General works |
| .5 | Forgeries |
| 61 | General special.  Civilization, culture, etc. |
| 62 | Special topics, A-Z |

| | |
|---|---|
| .A5 | Amulets |
| | Arrows, see .B6 |
| .A9 | Axes |
| | |
| .B3 | Baths |
| | Boats, see .S55 |
| .B5 | Board games |
| .B6 | Bows and arrows |
| | |
| | Canes, see .W34 |
| .C3 | Canopic jars |
| .C48 | Chariots |
| .C64 | Coffins |
| | |
| | Funeral customs, see .T6 |
| .L34 | Lamps |
| .M5 | Metals |
| .M58 | Mirrors |
| .M7 | Mummies |
| | |
| .O2 | Obelisks |
| .O88 | Ostraka |

                    Cf. PJ1675, Hieratic literature
                         PJ1829, Demotic literature

**Egypt**
  **Antiquities**
    **By period**
      **Ancient Egypt. Egyptology**

62                 Special topics, A-Z - Continued

         .P72    Pottery
               Pyramids, <u>see</u> DT63+
         .Q8     Quarries

         .S3     Scarabs
         .S55    Ships. Boats
         .S67    Sparterie
         .S7     Sphinxes
         .S73    Spoons
         .S8     Steles

               Temples, <u>see</u> DT68.8
         .T45    Tiles
         .T5     Toilet articles
         .T6     Tombs. Funeral customs
                 For tomb of Tutankhamen, <u>see</u> DT87.5
         .T65    Tools

         .U84    Ushabti
         .V47    Vessels
         .W34    Walking sticks. Canes

       Pyramids
63          General works
  .5           Pamphlets, etc.
64       Pamphlets, etc.
65       Public and political antiquities
66       Private antiquities
       Religious antiquities
         Cf. BL2428+, Egyptian mythology
68       General works
       Cultus
  .2          General works
  .3          Cult of the pharaohs
  .4        Festivals
  .8        Temples, altars, etc.
          Cf. NA215+, Egyptian architecture

**Egypt**

  **Antiquities**

    **By period** - Continued

69       Christian period

        Cf. BR130+, Christian religious antiquities

.5       Islamic period.   Islamic antiquities

70    Social life and Customs.  Civilization.

    Intellectual life

      Cf. DT61, Ancient Egyptian civilization

  Ethnography

71    General works

72    Individual elements in the population, A-Z

      .A73   Arameans

      .A75   Armenians

      .B4    Bedouins

      .C53   Circassians

      .C7    Copts

      .F4    French

      .G4    Germans

      .G7    Greeks

      .I8    Italians

      .K8    Kukus

      .S9    Syrians

73    Local Antiquities, A-Z

      .A13   Abū Jirāb

      .A14   Abū Ṣīr Site

      .A15   Abū Sunbul

      .A16   Abydos

      .A28   Akhmīm

      .A3    Al-Mina

      .A4    Alexandria

      .A7    Antinoopolis

Egypt
  Antiquities
73       ~~Local~~ antiquities, A-Z - Continued

|  |  |
|---|---|
| .A75 | Aphroditopolis |
| .A8 | Armant |
| .A812 | Arminna West (Site) |
| .A8127 | Arsinoe |
| .A813 | Arsinoites |
| .A82 | al'Asāsīf |
| .A85 | el Ashmūnein.  Hermopolis Magna |
| .A88 | Aswan |
| .A92 | Asyut Province |
| .A95 | 'Ayn Wāqifah Site |
| .B3 | Bacchis |
| .B33 | Bahariya Oasis |
| .B4 | Beni Hasan (Bani or Beni Hassan) |
| .B44 | Biban el Moluk.  Valley of the Kings |
| .B8 | Bubastis S |
| .C44 | Cellia (Monastery) |
| .C55 | Clysma |
| .D25 | ad Dab'ah |
| .D3 | Dahshur |
| .D33 | Dakhla Oasis |
| .D4 | Dandara |
|  | Dayr al-Madinah Site, <u>see</u> .D47 |
| .D45 | Deir el-Bahrr (Temple) |
| .D47 | Deir el-Medina |
| .D48 | Deir el-Shelwit Site |
| .D49 | Dendūr |
| .D492 | el-Derr.  Rock Temple of el-Derr |
| .D56 | Dionysias.  Qasr Qarun |
| .E43 | El-Kab |
| .E45 | Elephantine |
| .F38 | Fayyūm |
| .G47 | Gerf Hussein (Temple) |
| .G5 | Gizeh |
| .G85 | Gurob |

Egypt
  Antiquities
73      Local Antiquities, A-Z - Continued

   .H25   Haram Zāwiyat al 'Urbān
   .H34   Hawawish Site
   .H42   Heliopolis
   .H44   Heracleopolis Magna
   .H45   Hermopolite Nome
   .H57   Ḥisn, Kawm al- (Egypt)

   .I25   Ibis Nome
   .I3    Idfū
   .I46   Imlīḥīyah, Tall
   .I8    Isnā (Site)

   .K28   Kahun
   .K33   Karanis
   .K4    Karnak.   Temple of Ammon
   .K45   Kawa

   .K453  al Kawm al Ahmar.  Hierakonpolis
   .K47   Kellia Site
   .K5    Kharga (Oasis)
         Koptos, see .Q54
   .K8    Kush

   .L33   El Lāhūn
   .L47   el-Lessiya
   .L6    Lisht

   .M23   Madīnat Wāṭifah, Kwan
   .M24   Malkata Site
   .M245  Marea
   .M3    Medinet-Abu
   .M35   Medinet Madi.   Narmouthis

   .M5    Memphis
   .M54   Mendes
   .M75   Minyā (Province)
   .M8    Moeris (Lake)

Egypt
   Antiquities
73       Local Antiquities, A-Z - Continued

       .N2   Naga-ed Dêr
       .N26  Naqādah
             Narmouthis, <u>see</u> .M35
       .N28  Naṭrūn Valley

       .O8   Oxyrhynchus
       .P5   Philae
       .P58  Pi-Ramesse
       .P8   Ptolemais

       .Q35  Qasr al-Sagha Region.   Temple of Qasr al-Sagha
       .Q54  Qifṭ.  Koptos
       .Q75  el-Qurna
       .Q76  Qurnat Murā'i Hill
       .Q77  Qusayr al-Qadīm

       .R5   Rizeiqāt
              Rock Temple of el-Derr, <u>see</u> .D492
       .S3   Sakkara
       .S38  Sayyālah

       .T2   Tanis
       .T23  Taphis
       .T24  el-Tarif Site
       .T25  Tell el-Amarna
              Temple of Qasr al-Sagha, <u>see</u> .Q35
              Thebes.   Temple of Luxor
       .T3     General works
       .T32    Memnon statue.  Mortuary Temple of
                 Amenhotep III
       .T33    Ramesseum
       .T85  Tūnat al-Jabal Site
              Valley of the Kings, <u>see</u> .B44
       .Z35  Zawiyat...

   History
74      Dictionaries.  Chronological tables, outlines, etc.
76      Biography (Collective)
         For individual biography, <u>see</u> the specific period,
           reign, or place
     Historiography
.7      General works
     Biography
.8       Collective
.9       Individual, A-Z

                            **Egypt**

                               **History** - Continued

                                    Study and teaching

                                          Class catalogs of audiovisual materials in

                                              .Z9A-Z

| | |
|---|---|
| 76.93 | General works |
| .95 | By region or country, A-Z |
| |     Subarranged by author |
| 77 | General works |
| 79 | Pamphlets, etc. |
| | General special |
| 80 |     General works |
| 81 |     Military history |
| |     Political and diplomatic history.  Foreign and general relations |
| 82 |       General works |
| .5 |       Relations with individual countries, A-Z |
| |         For list of countries, <u>see</u> pp. 212-214 |
| | **By period** |
| | **Ancient and early to 638 A.D.** |
| 83 |     General works |
| .A2 |       Through 1800 |
| |         e. g. Manetho |
| .A3-Z |       1801- |
| |     Old and middle kingdoms, 1st-17th dynasties, 3400-1580 B.C. |
| 85 |       General works |
| 86 |       Hyksos |
| |     18th-20th dynasties, 1580-1150 B.C. |
| 87 |       General works |
| .15 |       Hatshepsut, 1503-1482 |
| .2 |       Thutmose III, 1479-1447.  Megiddo |
| |       Amenhetep IV, 1375-1358 (Ikhnaton) |
| .4 |         General works |
| .45 |         Nefertete (Nofretete, Nefertiti), Consort of Amenhetep IV |
| .5 |       Tutenkhamun, 1358-1350 |
| 88 |       Rameses II, 1292-1225 |
| .5 |       Period of Jewish captivity |
| |         For history of the Jews, <u>see</u> DS121.5 |
| .8 |       Rameses III, 1198-1167 |

                         Egypt
                           History
                             By period
                               Ancient and early to 638 A.D. - Continued
89                                 1150-663 B.C., 21st-24th dynasties
90                                 663-525 B.C., 25th-26th dynasties
91                                 Persian rule, 525-332 B.C.
                                   Alexander and Ptolemies, 332-30 B.C.
92                                   General works
  .A2                                  Through 1800
  .A3-Z                                1801-
  .7                                   Cleopatra
                                   Roman rule, 30 B.C.-638 A.D.
93                                   General works
  .A2                                  Through 1800
  .A3-Z                                1801-
                             Modern
94                               General works
                                 Moslems, 638-1798
95                                 General works
                                   638-1250
  .5                                 General works
  .55                                Conquest. Omayyads. Abbasids, 638-868
                                     Tulūnids, 868-905
  .6                                   General works
  .64                                  Biography and memoirs
                                         .A2A-Z  Collective
                                         .A3-Z   Individual, A-Z
                                     Ikhshīdids, 935-969.  Interregnum, 905-935
  .65                                  General works
  .69                                  Biography and memoirs
                                         .A2A-Z  Collective
                                         .A3-Z   Individual, A-z
                                     Fatimids, 909-1171
  .7                                   General works
  .78                                  Biography and memoirs
                                         .A2A-Z  Collective
                                         .A3-Z   Individual, A-Z
                                     Ayyūbids, 1169-1250
  .8                                    General works
  .88                                   Biography and memoirs
                                          .A2A-Z  Collective
                                          .A3-Z   Individual, A-Z

           **Egypt**
             **History**
               **By period**
                 **Modern**
                    Moslems, 638-1798 - Continued
                      1250-1517.  Mamelukes

|        |   |
|--------|---|
| 96     | General works |
| .3     | Biography and memoirs |
|        |   .A2A-Z  Collective |
|        |   .A3-Z   Individual, A-Z |
|        | By period |
| .4     | Bahri line, 1250-1390 |
| .7     | Burji line, 1382-1517 |
|        | 1517-1798.  Turkish rule |
| 97     | General works |
| 98.5   | Ali Bey, 1766-1773 |
|        | 1798-1879.  19th century |
| 100    | General works |
| 102    | Biography and memoirs |
|        |   .A2A-Z  Collective |
|        |   .A3-Z   Individual, A-Z |
|        |   |
|        |     .S2  Salt, Henry |
|        |   |
| 103    | 1798-1805 |
|        |   Cf. DC225+, French expedition to Egypt |
| 104    | Mohammed Ali, 1805-1848 |
| .5     | Ibrahim, 1848 |
| .7     | Abbas I, 1848-1854 |
| 105    | Mohammed Said, 1854-1863 |
| 106    | Ismail, 1863-1879 |
|        | 1879-1952 |
|        | For Sudan, <u>see</u> DT154.1+ |
| 107    | General works |
| .2     | Biography and memoirs |
|        |   .A2A-Z  Collective |
|        |   .A3-Z   Individual, A-Z |
|        |   |
|        |     .A5  Ahmad Seif-ed Din, Prince |
|        |     .B16 Baker, Sir Samuel White |
|        |   |
|        |     .C7  Cromer, Evelyn Baring, 1st Earl of |
|        |   |
|        |     .T3  Taha Husayn |

Egypt
  History
    By period
      Modern
        1879-1952 - Continued
          Tewfik, 1879-1892

| | |
|---|---|
| 107.3 | General works |
| .4 | Arabi Pasha, 1882 |
| .6 | Abbas II (Abbas Hilmi), 1892-1914 |
| .7 | Hussein Kamil, 1914-1917 |
| .8 | Fuad I, 1917-1936 |
| .82 | Faruq I, 1936-1952 |
| | Republic, 1952- |
| .821 | Periodicals. Societies. Serials |
| .822 | Congresses |
| .823 | Sources and documents |
| .824 | Historiography |
| .825 | General works |
| .8255 | Addresses, essays, lectures |
| .826 | Social life and customs. Civilization. Intellectual life |
| .8265 | Military history |
| .827 | Political history |
| .8275 | Foreign and general relations |
| .828 | Biography and memoirs |
| |   .A2A-Z Collective |
| |   .A3-Z Individual, A-Z |
| | By period |
| .83 | Nasser, Gamal Abdel, 1952-1970 |
| .85 | Sadat, Anwar, 1970-1981 |
| .87 | 1981- |

**Local history and description**
  Nile River (General)
    For the Nile River in individual countries, <u>see</u> the country, e. g. DT159.6.N54, Sudan

| | |
|---|---|
| 115 | General works |
| 116 | Nile in Egypt |
| 117 | Sources of the Nile |
| | Cf. DT361+, Ruwenzori Mountains |

```
                    Egypt
                       Local history and description - Continued
        137                Governorships, provinces, regions, etc., A-Z

                                e. g.  .B8    al-Buḥayrah

                                       .D26   Damietta region
                                       .G5    al-Gharbīyah

                                              Nubia, see DT159.6.N83
                                              Sinai Peninsula, see DS110.5

                                       .T3    Taḥrīr (Province)
                                       .W4    Western Desert
                          Cities, towns, etc.
                            Cairo
        139                   Periodicals.  Societies.  Serials
        141                   Directories.  Dictionaries.  Gazetteers
        142                   Guidebooks
        143                   General works
                              Description and travel
        144                     General works
          .2                      Early and medieval
          .3                    Views
        145                   Antiquities
        146                   Social life and customs.  Civilization.
                                Intellectual life
                              History
        147                     Biography (Collective)
                                  For individual biography, see the specific
                                    period, reign, or place
        148                     General works
                                By period
        149                       Early and medieval
                              Sections, districts, suburbs, etc.
        150                     Collective
          .5                    Individual, A-Z
                              Monuments, statues, etc.
        151                     Collective
          .5                    Individual, A-Z
                              Buildings
        153                     Collective
          .5                    Individual, A-Z
```

**Egypt**
**Local history and description**
Cities, towns, etc. - Continued
154　　　　　Other cities, towns, etc., A-Z
For extinct cities, towns, and archaeological
sites, see DT73
e. g.　.A4　Alexandria

.H5　Helwan
.K6　Kharga (Oasis)

.P7　Port Said

.S5　Siwa (Oasis)
.S9　Suez (Isthmus and Canal)


## SUDAN.　ANGLO-EGYPTIAN SUDAN

154.1　　　Periodicals.　Societies.　Serials
Museums, exhibitions, etc.
.2　　　　General works
.25　　　　Individual.　By place, A-Z
.3　　　Congresses
.32　　　Sources and documents
Collected works (nonserial)
.33　　　　Several authors
.34　　　　Individual authors
.4　　　Gazetteers.　Dictionaries, etc.
.45　　　Directories
.5　　　Guidebooks
.6　　　General works
.65　　　General special
.67　　　Views
.68　　　Historic monuments, landmarks, scenery, etc. (General)
For local, see DT159.6+
.69　　　Historical geography
Description and travel
.7　　　　History of travel
.72　　　　Early through 1800
.73　　　　19th century
.74　　　　20th century through 1955
.75　　　　1956-

**Sudan. Anglo-Egyptian Sudan** - Continued

| | |
|---|---|
| 154.8 | Antiquities |
| | For local antiquities, <u>see</u> DT159.6+ |
| .9 | Social life and customs. Civilization. Intellectual life |
| | For specific periods, <u>see</u> the period or reign |
| | Ethnography |
| 155 | General works |
| .2 | Individual elements in the population, A-Z |

| | |
|---|---|
| .A35 | Acoli |
| .A53 | Amaa |
| .A68 | Anuaks |
| .A78 | Arabs (General) |
| .A79 | Atuot |
| .A93 | Azande |
| | |
| .B34 | Baggara |
| .B44 | Beja |
| .B47 | Berti |
| .B65 | Bongo |
| | |
| .D36 | Danagla |
| .D53 | Didinga |
| .D56 | Dinka |
| | |
| .G74 | Greeks |
| .H38 | Hausas |
| .J33 | Ja'aliyyīn |
| .K32 | Kababish |
| .K74 | Kreish |
| | |
| .L86 | Luo |
| .M36 | Mandari |
| .M87 | Murle |
| | |
| .N55 | Nilotic tribes (General) |
| .N82 | Nuba |
| | Nubians, <u>see</u> DT159.6.N83 |
| .N85 | Nuer |
| | |
| .R37 | Rashayidah |
| .R83 | Rufa'a al-Hoi |
| .S45 | Shaikia |
| .S46 | Shilluks |
| .U38 | Uduk |

                   **Sudan.   Anglo-Egyptian Sudan** - Continued
                      **History**
                          Periodicals.   Societies.   Serials, <u>see</u> DT154.1

155.3                Dictionaries.   Chronological tables, outlines, etc.
                          Biography (Collective)
                             For individual biography, <u>see</u> the specific
                               period, reign, or place
     .4                    General works
     .42                 Rulers, kings, etc.
                       Houses, noble families, etc.
     .44                   General works
     .45                   Individual houses, families, etc., A-Z
     .46               Statesmen
                       Historiography
     .5                  General works
                       Biography of historians, area studies specialists,
                          archaeologists, etc.
     .52                   Collective
     .53                   Individual, A-Z
                       Study and teaching
     .55                  General works
     .56                  By region or country, A-Z
                            Subarranged by author
                     General works
     .58                  Through 1800
     .6                  1801-
     .62                 Addresses, essays, lectures.   Anecdotes, etc.
                     General special
     .64                 Military history
                          For individual campaigns and engagements, <u>see</u>
                             the special period or reign
     .7                  Political history
                          For specific periods, <u>see</u> the period or reign
                     Foreign and general relations
                       Class general works on the diplomatic history
                         of a period with the period, e. g. DT157.6.
                         For works on relations with a specific
                         country regardless of period, <u>see</u> DT155.9
     .78                 Sources and documents
     .8                  General works
     .9                  Relations with individual countries, A-Z
                        For list of countries, <u>see</u> pp. 218-220

            **Sudan.   Anglo-Egyptian Sudan**
              **History** - Continued
                  **By period**

| | |
|---|---|
| 156 | Early to 641 |
| .3 | 641-1820 |
| | 1821- |
| .4 | General works |
| | 19th century |
| .5 | General works |
| .6 | 1881-1899. Mahdiyah. Gordon. Kitchener |
| | Cf. DT363, Emin Pasha |
| .7 | 1900-1955 |
| | Republic, 1956- |
| 157 | Periodicals. Societies. Serials |
| .1 | Congresses |
| .2 | Sources and documents |
| .23 | Collected works (Nonserial) |
| .25 | Historiography |
| .3 | General works |
| .33 | General special |
| .36 | Addresses, essays, lectures |
| .4 | Social life and customs. Civilization. |
| | Intellectual life |
| .43 | Military history |
| .5 | Political history |
| .6 | Foreign and general relations |
| | Biography and memoirs |
| .63 | Collective |
| .65 | Individual, A-Z |
| .67 | Civil War, 1956-1972. Southern Sudan |
| | question |

        **Local history and description**

| | |
|---|---|
| 159.6 | Provinces, regions, etc., A-Z |

                e. g.    .B34   Bahr al Ghazal (Province)
                             .D27   Darfur
                             .K67   Kordofan

                             .N54   an Nil al Azraq
                             .N83   Nubia
                                       Including Egyptian Nubia

                           .S46   Sennar
                           .S73   Southern Region

        Sudan.   Anglo-Egyptian Sudan
          Local history and description - Continued
            Cities, towns, etc.
159.7           Khartum.   Greater Khartum
    .9           Other cities, towns, etc., A-Z

                    e. g.   .A35   Akashah Site
                            .A37   Aksha

                            .B45   Begrawia Site
                            .B85   Buhen
                            J32    Jabal Mayyah Site
                            .K37   Karmah
                            .L55   Lion Temple of Naq'a

                            .M47   Meroe
                            .M57   Mirgissa


                    NORTH AFRICA

            Including Egypt and Maghrib (Collectively)

160           Periodicals.   Societies.   Serials
162           General works
              Description and travel
163             Early through 1800
                    Cf. DG59.A4, Roman provinces of Africa
164             1801-1900
165             1901-1950
    .2          1951-
    .9          Pamphlets, etc.
              Ethnography, see DT193+
              History
167             General works
                By period
                  Carthaginian period
                      Cf. DG241+, Roman conquest, 264-133, B.C.
                      For woks on Carthage and its Empire, see
                        DT269.C3+
168               General works
169               General special
    .5            Pamphlets, etc.

      North Africa
        History
          By period - Continued

| | |
|---|---|
| 170 | Roman period, 146 B.C.-439 A.D. |
| 171 | Vandals, 439-534 |
| |     Cf. D139, Migrations |
| 172 | Byzantine period |
| 173 | Arab conquest (to ca. 1516 or 1524) |
| 174 | 16th-18th centuries |
| 176 | 19th-20th centuries |
| 177 | Other |

## NORTHWEST AFRICA

      Including Maghrib, Mali, Mauretania and
        other Sahara countries west of Libya
        (Collectively)

| | |
|---|---|
| 179.2 | Periodicals. Societies. Serials |
| .3 | Guidebooks. Gazetteers |
| .4 | General works |
| .5 | Description and travel |
| .6 | Antiquities |
| .7 | Social life and customs. Civilization. Intellectual life |
| .8 | Ethnology |
| .9 | History |

## MAGHRIB. BARBARY STATES

      Including Libya, Tunisia, Algeria and Morocco
        (Collectively)

| | |
|---|---|
| 181 | Periodicals. Societies |
| .5 | Congresses |
| 182 | Collections |
| 183 | Biography (Collective) |
| 184 | Guidebooks. Gazetteers. Directories, etc. |
| 185 | General works |

**Maghrib. Barbary States** - Continued

    Descritpion and travel

| | |
|---|---|
| 188 | Early through 1800 |
| 189 | 1801-1900 |
| 190 | 1901-1950 |
| .2 | 1951- |
| 191 | Antiquities |
| 192 | Social life and customs.  Civilization.  Intellectual life |

    Ethnography

| | |
|---|---|
| 193 | General works |
| .5 | Individual elements in the population, A-Z |

          .B45    Berbers

*193.95*   *Historiograph*

**History**

| | |
|---|---|
| 194 | General works |
| | Political and diplomatic history.  Foreign and general relations |
| 197 | General works |
| .5 | Relations with individual countries, A-Z |
| |     For list of countries, <u>see</u> pp. 212-214 |

    By period

| | |
|---|---|
| 198 | Early to 647 |
| 199 | 647-1516 |
| | 1516-1830.  Period of piracy |
| |     For relations with the United States, <u>see</u> E335 |
| 201 | General works |
| 202 | 16th century |
| 204 | 19th-20th centuries |

**Libya (Tripoli)**

| | |
|---|---|
| 211 | Periodicals.  Societies |
| 212 | Collections |
| 213 | Biography (Collective) |
| 214 | Guidebooks.  Gazetteers |
| 215 | General works |

    Description and travel

| | |
|---|---|
| 218 | Early through 1800 |
| 219 | 1801-1900 |
| 220 | 1901-1950 |
| .2 | 1951- |

**Maghrib.   Barbary States**
Libya (Tripoli) - Continued

| | |
|---|---|
| 221 | Antiquities |
| 222 | Social life and customs.   Civilization.   Intellectual life |
| | Ethnography |
| 223 | General works |
| .2 | Individual elements in the population, A-Z |

.B43   Bedouins

.T85   Turks

.Z87   Zuwaya

**History**

| | |
|---|---|
| .3 | Dictionaries.   Chronological tables, etc. |
| | Historiography |
| .6 | General works |
| .8 | Biography |
| | .A2A-Z   Collective |
| | .A3-Z    Individual, A-Z |
| 224 | General works |
| | Political and diplomatic history.   Foreign and general relations |
| 227 | General works |
| .5 | Relations with individual countries, A-Z |

For list of countries, see pp. 218-220

By period

| | |
|---|---|
| 228 | Early to 642 |
| 229 | 642-1551 |
| | 1551-1912 |
| 231 | General works |
| | War with the United States, <u>see</u> E335 |
| | 1801-1912 |
| 233 | General works |
| | War with the United States, <u>see</u> E335 |
| 234 | Turco-Italian War, 1911-1912 |
| 235 | 1912-1951 |
| .5 | 1951-1969 |
| 236 | 1969- |

                    **Maghrib.   Barbary States**
                      **Libya (Tripoli) - Continued**
                        **Local history and description**
238                       Provinces, regions, etc., A-Z
                              e. g.          Barqah, <u>see</u> .C8

                                        .C8  Cyrenaica.  Barqah

                                        .F5  Fezzan

                                        .S3  Sahara
                                        .T5  Tibesti Mountains
                                                 Cf. DT546.4+, Chad
                                        .T8  Tripolitania

239                           Cities, towns, etc., A-Z

                              e. g.   .C9    Cyrene
                                      .D4    Derna

                                      .J35   Jarmah
                                      .J4    Jebel Nefusa

                                      .S115  Sabratha

                                      .T6    Tolemaide
                                      .T7    Tripoli


                    **Tunisia (Tunis)**
241                     Periodicals.  Societies
242                     Collections
243                     Biography (Collective)
244                     Guidebooks.  Gazetteers.  Directories, etc.
245                     General works
247.9                   Historical geography
                        Description and travel
248                        Early through 1800
249                        1801-1900
250                        1901-1950
   .2                      1951-
251                     Antiquities
252                     Social life and customs.  Civilization.  Intellectual
                             life

Maghrib.  Barbary States
  Tunisia (Tunis) - Continued
    Ethnography
253      General works
.2      Individual elements in the population, A-Z

      .A43  Algerians

      .I8   Italians

      .M8   Moriscos

      .N65  Nomads

**History**
  Historiography
.4      General works
.5      Biography of historians
      .A2A-Z  Collective
      .A3-Z   Individual, A-Z
254     General works
    Political and diplomatic history.  Foreign and general relations
257     General works
.5     Relations with individual countries, A-Z
     For list of countries, see pp. 218-220
**By period**
258     Early to 647
259     647-1516
    1516-1830.  Period of piracy
261      General works
262      16th century
      Including Siege of Goletta, 1573
    1830-1881.  19th century
263      General works
     Biography and memoirs
.75     Collective
.76     Individual, A-Z
    French Protectorate, 1881-1957
.9     Periodicals.  Societies.  Serials
.95     Sources and documents
264     General works
.25     Social life and customs.  Civilization. Intellectual life

                   Maghrib.  Barbary States
                     Tunisia (Tunis)
                       History
                         By period
                           French Protectorate, 1881-1957 - Continued

264.26                    Military and naval history
  .27                   Political history
  .28                   Foreign and general relations
                           Biography and memoirs
  .29                     Collective
  .3                     Individual, A-Z

                               e. g.   .B6  Bourguiba, Habib, 1903-

                                      .L3  Lakdar, Mohamed

                           Republic, 1957-
  .35                   Periodicals.  Societies.  Serials
  .36                   Congresses
  .37                   Sources and documents
  .38                   Collected works (nonserial)
  .39                   Historiography
  .4                    General works
  .42                   General special
  .43                   Addresses, essays, lectures
  .44                   Social life and customs.  Civilization.
                            Intellectual life
  .45                   Military and naval history
  .46                   Political history
  .47                   Foreign and general relations
                           Biography and memoirs
  .48                   Collective
  .49                   Individual, A-Z

              **Local history and description**
268                 Districts, regions, etc., A-Z

                    e. g.       Jarbah, <u>see</u> .J4
                           .J4  Jerba.  Jarbah

                           .N4  Nefzaoua

Maghrib.  Barbary States
  Tunisia (Tunis)
    **Local history and description** - Continued
269        Cities, towns, etc., A-Z

          e. g.  .A48  Althiburos (Tunisia)
                .B37  Belalis Maior
                .B6   Bizerta
                .B85  Bulla Regia

                       Carthage.  Carthaginian Empire
                          Cf. DG225.C37, Carthaginians
                              in Italy
              .C3     Periodicals.  Societies.  Serials
              .C32    General works
              .C33    Antiquities
              .C34    Social life and customs.
                         Civilization.  Intellectual life
              .C35    History
                       For Punic wars, <u>see</u> DG242+
              .C38    Carthaginian (Punic) colonies
                      (Collectively)

              .H3     Hammamet

              .K3     Kairwan
              .K37    Kerkouane
               .K4     Khumir

              .M28    Mactaris
              .M6     Monastir
              .M87    Musti

              .R35    Raqqada
              .S4     Ṣafāqis.  Sfax

              .T8     Tunis

              .U73    Ureu
              .U8     Utica

**Maghrib. Barbary States** - Continued
    **Algeria**

| | |
|---|---|
| 271 | Periodicals.  Societies |
| | Museums, exhibitions, etc. |
| .2 | General works |
| .3 | Individual.  By place, A-Z |
| 272 | Collections |
| 273 | Biography (Collective) |
| 274 | Guidebooks.  Gazetteers.  Directories, etc. |
| 275 | General works |
| 276 | Views |
| | Description and travel |
| 277.8 | History of travel |
| 278 | Early through 1800 |
| 279 | 1801-1900 |
| 280 | 1901-1950 |
| .2 | 1951- |
| 281 | Antiquities |
| 282 | Social life and customs.  Civilization.  Intellectual life |
| | For specific periods, <u>see</u> the period or reign |
| | Ethnography |
| 283 | General works |
| | Individual elements in the population |
| | Berbers |
| .2 | General works |
| .3 | Individual groups, A-Z |
| | Kabyles, <u>see</u> DT298.K2 |
| | Arabs |
| .4 | General works |
| .5 | Individual groups, A-Z |
| .6 | Other, A-Z |
| | .A44  Ajjer |
| | .F7  French.  Pieds noirs |
| | .I73  Italians |
| | .M35  Maltese |
| | .N6  Nomads |
| | .P64  Poles |
| | .S62  Spaniards |
| | .T83  Tuaregs |

Maghrib. Barbary States
Algeria - Continued
History
283.7        Dictionaries.  Chronological tables, etc.
             Historiography
  .8           General works
             Biography
  .9             Collective
  .92            Individual, A-Z
284        General works
285        General special
           Political and diplomatic history.  Foreign and
               general relations
287          General works
  .5         Relations with individual countries, A-Z
                 For list of countries, see pp. 212-214

           By period
288          Early to 647
289          647-1516
             1516-1830.  Period of piracy
291            General works
292            16th century
             1830-1901
294            General works
             War with the United States, see E335
             1901-1945
  .5           General works
  .7           Biography and memoirs
                 .A1A-Z  Collective
                 :A2-Z   Individual, A-Z

                          .A3  'Abd-al-Ḵādir ibn Muḥyi
                               al-Dīn, Amir of Mascara

                          .E2  Eberhardt, Isabelle

                          .E8  Étienne, Eugène

                          .T5  Tidjani, Aurélie (Picard)

<pre>
                    Maghrib.  Barbary States
                       Algeria
                       History
                         By period - Continued
                           1945-1962
                               Including the Algerian Revolution, 1954-1962
       295                      General works
         .3                     Biography and memoirs
                                  .A1A-Z  Collective
                                  .A2-Z   Individual, A-Z

                                          .B6  Boupacha, Djamila

                           1962-
         .5                     General works
         .55                    Biography and memoirs
                                  .A1A-Z  Collective
                                  .A2-Z   Individual, A-Z
       296                 Other
                       Local history and description
       298                 Departments, regions, etc., A-Z

                                  e. g.  .C7  Constantine
                                         .E7  Erg, El

                                         .K2  Kabylia (Great Little)

                                         .O8  Oran

                                         .S6  Southern Territories

       299                 Cities, towns, etc., A-Z

                                  e. g.  .A5  Algiers

                                         .B5  Biskra
                                         .B7  Bougie

                                         .C5  Cherchel
                                         .C6  Constantine
                                         .N35 Nādōr Site
                                         .O7  Oran

                                              Thamugadi City, see .T5
                                         .T5  Timgad

                                         .T55 Tlemcen
                                         .T7  Touggourt.  Tuggurt
                                              Tuggurt, see .T7
</pre>

**Maghrib. Barbary States - Continued**
    **Morocco**

| | |
|---|---|
| 301 | Periodicals. Societies |
| 302 | Collections |
| 303 | Biography (Collective) |
| 304 | Guidebooks. Gazetteers. Directories, etc. |
| 305 | General works |
| | Description and travel |
| 307 | History of travels |
| 308 | Early through 1800 |
| 309 | 1801-1900 |
| 310 | 1901-1950 |
| .2 | 1951- |
| 311 | Antiquities |
| 312 | Social life and customs. Civilization. Intellectual life |
| | Ethnography |
| 313 | General works |
| | Individual elements in the population |
| | Berbers |
| .2 | General works |
| .3 | Individual groups, A-Z |

        .A35 Ahansala
        .A37 Ait Atta
        .A93 Ayash

        Beni Urriaghel, _see_ .W34
        .B46 Beni Zerual

        .I65 Iqar'iyen
        .N4 Ndhir

        .R53 Rif
        .S44 Seksawa

        .W34 Waryaghar. Beni Urriaghel

    Arabs

| .4 | General works |
| .5 | Individual groups, A-Z |

        .U4 Ulad Stut

| .6 | Others, A-Z |

         **Maghrib. Barbary States**
           **Morocco** - Continued
             **History**

| | |
|---|---|
| 313.7 | Dictionaries. Chronological tables, outlines, etc. |
| .75 | Biography (Collective) |
| | Historiography |
| .8 | General works |
| | Biography of historians |
| .82 | Collective |
| .83 | Individual, A-Z |
| 314 | General works |
| 315 | General special |
| | Political and diplomatic history. Foreign and general relations |
| | For special periods, reigns, etc., <u>see</u> DT318+ |
| .5 | Relations with individual countries, A-Z |
| | For list of countries, <u>see</u> pp. 212-214 |
| | **By period** |
| 318 | Early to 647. Mauretania |
| 319 | 647-1516 |
| | 1516-1830. Period of piracy |
| 321 | General works |
| 322 | 16th century |
| 323.5 | Ismail, 1672-1727 |
| | 1830-1955 |
| 324 | General works |
| | Biography and memoirs |
| .9 | Collective |
| .92 | Individual, A-Z |

                  e. g.   .A3  Abd el-Krim, 1883-1963

                         .M6  Muḥammad V, <u>King of Morocco</u>, 1909-1963

| | |
|---|---|
| | 1955 |
| 325 | Periodicals. Societies. Serials |
| .1 | Congresses |
| .2 | Sources and documents |
| .23 | Collected works (nonserial) |
| .3 | Historiography |

Maghrib.   Barbary States
   Morocco
      History
         By period
            1955 - Continued

| | |
|---|---|
| 325.4 | General works |
| .42 | General special |
| .45 | Addresses, essays, lectures |
| .5 | Social life and customs.  Civilization.  Intellectual life |
| .6 | Military history |
| .7 | Political history |
| .8 | Foreign and general relations |
| | Biography and memoirs |
| .9 | Collective |
| .92 | Individual, A-Z |

                e. g.   .B55  Bin Barakah, al-Mahdi,
                                 1920-

                      .H37  Hassan II, <u>King of Morocco</u>,
                                 1929-

**Local history and description**

| | |
|---|---|
| 328 | Regions, islands, etc., A-Z |

                e. g.   .A8  Atlas Mountains

                      .P3  Peregil Island

                      .R5  Rif Mountains

| | |
|---|---|
| 329 | Cities, towns, etc., A-Z |

                e. g.   .A7  Arzila
                      .C3  Casablanca
                      .C5  Ceuta (Spain)

                      .L59 Lixus
                      .M3  Marrakesh

                      .S12 Safi
                      .T16 Tangier Zone.   International Zone
                      .T4  Tetuan

                      .V6  Volubilis

**Maghrib. Barbary States**
   **Morocco** - Continued

|       |                                                           |
|-------|-----------------------------------------------------------|
| 330   | Spanish Morocco                                           |
|       |    Including Ifni; Northern and Southern Zones |

**Sahara**
   Cf. DT548, West Sahara
      DT346.S7, Spanish Sahara

|       |                                                           |
|-------|-----------------------------------------------------------|
| 331   | Periodicals. Societies. Serials                          |
| 332   | Guidebooks. Gazetteers                                   |
| 333   | General works. History and description. Travel          |
| 335   | Antiquities                                              |
| 337   | Social life and customs. Civilization. Intellectual life |
| 339   | Other                                                    |
| 346   | Regions, tribes, etc., A-Z                               |

     .C5    Chaamba

     .D38   Daza

     .M4    Mekhadma

     .O8    Ouled Nail

            Rio de Oro, see .S7
            Sekia el Hamra, see .S7

     .S7    Spanish Sahara. Western Sahara. Rio de
            Oro. Sekia el Hamra

     .T4    ~~Tibbu~~ Teda. Tibbu

     .T7    Tuaregs
     .T8    Twat

            Western Sahara, see .S7

## CENTRAL SUB-SAHARAN AFRICA

Including Sahara to Congo basin, travel across
the continent by Congo and Lake Region, etc.,
to 1950, and biographies of explorers of the
region

Works by and about Sir Henry Morton Stanley    DT 351.S6

   .S6A3     Autobiography

   .S68-89   Other works

   .S9A-Z    Works about Stanley

For works by Theodore Roosevelt, see SK252

For works by and about David Livingstone, see
DT731.L7+

| | |
|---|---|
| 348 | Periodicals. Societies. Serials |
| 349 | Congresses |
| .2 | Sources and documents |
| | Collected works (nonserial) |
| .3 | Several authors |
| .4 | Individual authors |
| .5 | Gazetteers. Dictionaries, etc. |
| .6 | Place names (General) |
| .7 | Directories |
| .8 | Guidebooks |
| 351 | General works |
| .5 | Views |
| | Description and travel |
| | Early works through 1950, see DT351 |
| 352 | 1951-1980 |
| .2 | 1981- |
| .3 | Antiquities |
| .4 | Social life and customs. Civilization. Intellectual life |
| | Ethnography |
| .42 | General works |
| .43 | Individual elements in the population, A-Z |

    .E16   East Indians

**Central Sub-Saharan Africa** - Continued
    **History**
        Study and teaching, <u>see</u> DT19.8+

| | |
|---|---|
| 352.5 | General works |
| .6 | Biography and memoirs |
| | By period |
| .65 |     Early |
| .7 |     Colonial |
| .8 |     Independent |
| | Political and diplomatic history |
| 353 |     General works |
| .5 |     Relations with individual countries, A-Z |

                For list of countries, <u>see</u> pp. 212-214
    British Central Africa, <u>see</u> DT850+
    Wadai, <u>see</u> DT546.49.W33

| | |
|---|---|
| 356 | West Central Africa.  West Sudan |

        Including works by Paul Du Chaillu, Mungo Park,
           etc.
        Cf. DT470+, West coast and Guinea

| | |
|---|---|
| 360 | Niger River |

        Cf. DT470+, West Coast
           DT521+, French West Africa
           DT547+, French Niger
    Lake Chad, <u>see</u> DT546.49.L34

    East Central (Lake region)
        Including Ruwenzori Mountains (Mountains of
          the Moon)
        Cf. DT117, Sources of the Nile
           DT365+, East coast

| | |
|---|---|
| 361 | Description and travel |
| | History |
| |     Biography and memoirs |
| 362 |     Collective |
| 363 |     Emin Pasha.  Exploration and relief expedition |
| .2 |     Other individual, A-Z |
| .3 | General works |

## EASTERN AFRICA

| | |
|---|---|
| 365 | Periodicals. Societies. Serials |
| .13 | Sources and documents |
| .15 | Gazetteers. Dictionaries, etc. |
| .17 | Guidebooks |
| .18 | General works |
| .19 | Views |
| .2 | Description and travel |
| .3 | Antiquities |
| |     For local antiquities, <u>see</u> DT367+ |
| .4 | Social life and customs. Civilization. Intellectual life |
| |     For specific periods, <u>see</u> the period |
| | Ethnography |
| .42 |     General works |
| .45 |     Individual elements in the population, A-Z |
| |        .S93   Swahili-speaking peoples |
| | **History** |
| .5 |     General works |
| |     General special |
| .59 |       Political history |
| |         For specific periods, <u>see</u> the period |
| |       Foreign and general relations |
| |         Class general works on the diplomatic history of a period with the period, e. g. DT365.65+. For works on relations with a specific country regardless of period, <u>see</u> DT365.63 |
| .62 |         General works |
| .63 |         Relations with individual countries, A-Z |
| |           For list of countries, <u>see</u> pp. 212-214 |
| |     By period |
| .65 |       Early to 1884 |
| |       1884-1960 |
| .7 |         General works |
| |         Biography and memoirs |
| |           Class biography under individual country except for those persons who are associated with more than one country or who inhabited a region which does not correspond to a modern jurisdiction |
| .74 |           Collective |
| .75 |           Individual, A-Z |
| .8 |         1960- |

|        | **Eastern Africa** - Continued |
|--------|---------------------------------|
|        | **Northeast Africa** |
|        | Including Sudan, Ethiopia, Somalia and Djibouti |
|        | (Collectively) |
| 367    | Periodicals.  Societies.  Serials |
| .13    | Sources and documents |
| .17    | Guidebooks |
| .18    | General works |
| .19    | Views |
| .2     | Description and travel |
| .4     | Social life and customs.  Civilization.  Intellectual life |
|        | For specific periods, <u>see</u> the period |
|        | Ethnography |
| .42    | General works |
| .45    | Individual elements in the population, A-Z |
|        | **History** |
| .5     | General works |
|        | General special |
| .59    | Political history |
|        | For specific periods, <u>see</u> the period |
|        | Foreign and general relations |
|        | Class general works on the diplomatic history of a period with the period, e. g. DT367.65+. For works on relations with a specific country regardless of period, <u>see</u> DT367.63 |
| .62    | General works |
| .63    | Relations with individual countries, A-Z |
|        | For list of countries, <u>see</u> pp. 212-214 |
|        | **By period** |
| .65    | Early to 1900 |
|        | 1900-1974 |
| .75    | General works |
|        | Biography and memoirs |
|        | Class biography under individual country except for those persons who are associated with more than one country or who inhabited a region which does not correspond to a modern jurisdiction |
| .76    | Collective |
| .77    | Individual, A-Z |
| .8     | 1974- |
|        | Local history and description, <u>see</u> the individual country |

Eastern Africa - Continued
  Ethiopia (Abyssinia)

| | |
|---|---|
| 371 | Periodicals. Societies. Serials |
| .2 | Congresses |
| .5 | Gazetteers. Dictionaries, etc. |
| 373 | General works |
| 374 | General special |
| .3 | Views |
| | Description and travel |
| 375 | Early through 1400 |
| 376 | 1401-1700 |
| 377 | 1701-1900 |
| 378 | 1901-1950 |
| .2 | 1951-1980 |
| .3 | 1981- |
| 379 | Antiquities |
| .5 | Social life and customs. Civilization. Intellectual life |
| | Ethnography |
| 380 | General works |
| .4 | Individual elements in the population, A-Z |

.A43  Amharas
.A7  Armenians

.B45  Beja
.B6  Bogos

.D3  Dasanetch
.D57  Dizi
  Falashas, see DS135.E75

  Gallas, see DT390.G2
.G35  Gimiras
.G66  Gonga
.G72  Greeks
.G85  Gurages

.H33  Hadiya
.H36  Hamar

                          Eastern Africa
                            Ethiopia (Abyssinia)
                              Ethnography
380.4                             Individual elements in the population, A-Z –
                                      Continued

                                  .K45   Kemants
                                  .K65   Konsos

                                  .M3    Majangirs
                                  .M32   Male
                                  .M87   Muslims

                                  .N54   Nilotic peoples
                                  .N92   Nyangatom

                                  .S5    Sidamas
                                  .S65   Somalis
                                  .S94   Swedes

                                  .T54   Tigrinya

                              **History**
                                Historiography
        .5                          General works
                                    Biography of historians, area studies
                                        specialists, archaeologists, etc.
        .6                              Collective
        .62                             Individual, A-Z
                                Study and teaching
        .8                          General works
        .85                         By region or country, A-Z
        .9                          Individual schools, A-Z
381                             General works
382                             Pamphlets, etc.
                                Political and diplomatic history.   Foreign and
                                    general relations
        .3                          General works
        .5                          Relations with individual countries, A-Z
                                        For list of countries, <u>see</u> pp. 212-214
                              **By period**
383                             Early through 1500
384                             16th-18th centuries

```
                    Eastern Africa
                      Ethiopia (Abyssinia)
                        History
                          By period - Continued
                            19th-20th centuries
386                           General works
  .3                          Theodore II, 1855-1868
                              John IV, 1872-1889
  .7                            General works on life and reign
                                Biography and memoirs
  .72                             Collective
  .73                             Individual, A-Z
                              Menelik II, 1889-1913
387                             General works
  .3                            War with Italy, 1895-1896
  .5                          Lij Yasu, 1913-1916
  .6                          Waizeru Zauditu and Ras Taffari (Tafari)
                                Makonnen, 1916-1928

                              Haile Selassie I, 1928-1974
  .7                            General works
  .8                            Italo-Ethiopian War, 1935-1936
                                  .A1    Collections
                                         Documents
                                  .A2       League of Nations (as author)
                                  .A3-5     Italy
                                  .A6       Ethiopia
                                  .A7       Other countries, A-Z
                                  .A8-Z  General works.  By author
  .9                            1936-1974
  .92                           Biography and memoirs of contemporaries
                                  .A2A-Z  Collective
                                  .A3-Z   Individual, A-Z

                              1974-1991
  .95                            General works
  .952                           Somali-Ethiopian Conflict, 1977-
                                 Biography and memoirs
  .953                             Collective
  .954                             Individual, A-Z
```

**Eastern Africa**
  **Ethiopia (Abyssinia)** - Continued
390      Kingdoms, regions, cities, etc., A-Z

   e. g. .A3 Addis Ababa
         Aksum Kingdom, <u>see</u> .A88
      .A88 Axum. Aksum Kingdom

      .B5 Blue Nile

      .G2 Gallas (Galla, Oromo)
         Including territory

      .H3 Harar
      .K3 Kaffa (Kafa)

      .T5 Tigre
      .T8 Tsana (Tana) Lake

    **Eritrea**
392.8 391    Periodicals. Societies. Serials   &rarr; Guidebooks
   393    General works
    .4   Social life and customs. Civilization.
       Intellectual life
        For specific periods, <u>see</u> the period or
         reign
    .5   Ethnography

    **History**
394    General works
     By period
    .5   Early to 1890
395     1890-1941. Italian domination
    .3   1941-1952. British administration
        Including United Nations investigations
    .5   1952-1962. Federation with Ethiopia
397     1962-  . Annexation to Ethiopia
        Including civil war and liberation movements
398    Regions, cities, etc., A-Z

     e. g. .M3 Massaua (Massawa)

       .P8 Punt (Kingdom)

Eastern Africa - Continued
Somalia. Somaliland and adjacent territory
Including Italian and British Somaliland
Cf. DT391+, Eritrea
DT411+, French Territory of the Afars and
Issas; French Somaliland; Djibouti

| | |
|---|---|
| 401 | Periodicals. Societies. Serials |
| .13 | Congresses |
| .15 | Sources and documents |
| .2 | Gazetteers. Dictionaries, etc. |
| .4 | Guidebooks |
| .5 | General works |
| .6 | General special |
| .7 | Views |
| .8 | Description and travel |
| 402 | Antiquities |
| | For local antiquities, see DT409 |
| .2 | Social life and customs. Civilization. Intellectual life |
| | For specific periods, see the period or reign |
| | Ethnography |
| .3 | General works |
| .4 | Individual elements in the population, A-Z |
| | .R35 Rahanweyn |
| .45 | Somalis in foreign countries (General) |
| | For Somalis in a particular country, see the country |

**History**

| | |
|---|---|
| | Periodicals. Societies. Serials, see DT401 |
| .5 | Dictionaries. Chronological tables, outlines, etc. |
| .6 | Biography (Collective) |
| | For individual biography, see the specific period, reign, or place |
| .8 | Historiography |
| 403 | General works |
| .15 | Juvenile works |

Eastern Africa
  Somalia.  Somaliland and adjacent territory
   History - Continued
    General special

| | |
|---|---|
| 403.2 | General works |
| .25 | Political history |
| |    For specific periods, <u>see</u> the period or reign |
| | Foreign and general relations |
| |    Class general works on the diplomatic history of a period with the period, e. g. DT407+. For works on relations with a specific country regardless of period, <u>see</u> DT403.4 |
| .3 | General works |
| .4 | Relations with individual countries, A-Z |
| |    For list of countries, <u>see</u> pp. 212-214 |

    **By period**

| | |
|---|---|
| | Early to 1889 |
| |    Including Egyptian occupation and activities of the British East Africa Company |
| .5 | General works |
| | Biography and memoirs |
| .6 |    Collective |
| .7 |    Individual, A-Z |
| | 1885-1941.  British Somaliland.  British Protectorate |
| 404 | General works |
| | Biography and memoirs |
| .2 |    Collective |
| .3 |    Individual, A-Z |
| | 1889-1941.  Italian Somaliland |
| 405 | General works |
| | Biography and memoirs |
| .2 |    Collective |
| .3 |    Individual, A-Z |
| | 1941-1960.  British military administration. United Nations trusteeship |
| 406 | General works |
| | Biography and memoirs |
| .2 |    Collective |
| .3 |    Individual, A-Z |

Eastern Africa
   Somalia.   Somaliland and adjacent territory
      History
         By period - Continued
            1960-
                  For Somali-Ethiopian Conflict, <u>see</u> DT387.952
407                  General works
                  Biography and memoirs
   .2                   Collective
   .3                   Individual, A-Z
409            Local history and description, A-Z

            e. g.   .G58   Giuba, Italian Somaliland

                     Jubaland, <u>see</u> .G58

                     Oltre Giuba (Italian colony), <u>see</u>
                        .G58

      Djibouti.   French Territory of the Afars and Issas.
         French Somaliland
411         Periodicals.  Societies.  Serials
   .13         Sources and documents
   .15         Gazetteers.  Dictionaries, etc.
   .2         Guidebooks
   .22         General works
   .24         Views
   .27         Description and travel
   .4         Social life and customs.  Civilization.  Intellectual
               life
                  For specific periods, <u>see</u> the period
            Ethnography
   .42            General works
   .45            Individual elements in the population, A-Z
         History
   .5            General works
            General special
               Foreign and general relations
                  Class general works on the diplomatic history
                     of a period with the period, e. g. DT411.65+.
                     For works on relations with a specific
                     country regardless of period, <u>see</u> DT411.63
   .62            General works
   .63            Relations with individual countries, A-Z
                     For list of countries, <u>see</u> pp. 212-214

Eastern Africa
Djibouti. French Territory of the Afars and Issas.
French Somaliland
History - Continued
By period

| | |
|---|---|
| 411.65 | Early to 1883 |
| | 1883-1977 |
| .75 | General works |
| | Biography and memoirs |
| .76 | Collective |
| .77 | Individual, A-Z |
| | 1977-    . Independent |
| .8 | General works |
| | Biography and memoirs |
| .82 | Collective |
| .83 | Individual, A-Z |
| .9 | Local history and description, A-Z |

East Africa. British East Africa
Including Uganda, Kenya, and Tanzania (Collectively)

| | |
|---|---|
| 421 | Periodicals. Societies. Serials |
| .2 | Sources and documents |
| .5 | Gazetteers. Dictionaries, etc. |
| 422 | Guidebooks |
| 423 | General works |
| .5 | Views |
| | Description and travel |
| 424 | To 1800 |
| 425 | 1800-1950 |
| 426 | 1951-1980 |
| 427 | 1981- |
| 428 | Antiquities |
| .5 | Social life and customs. Civilization. Intellectual life |
| | For specific periods, see the period |
| | Ethnography |
| 429 | General works |
| .5 | Individual elements in the population, A-Z |

.E27  East Indians

.K35  Kalenjin

```
                    Eastern Africa
                      East Africa.   British East Africa - Continued
                            History
        430                     Biography (Collective)
                                    For individual biography see the specific
                                        period or place
                                Historiography
          .5                      General works
                                  Biography of historians, area studies specialists,
                                      archaeologists, etc.
          .6                          Collective
          .7                          Individual, A-Z
        431                     General works
        432                     General special
                                By period
                                    Early to 1960, see DT431
          .5                        1960-
                      Uganda
        433.2                   Periodicals.  Societies.  Serials
          .213                  Sources and documents
          .215                  Gazetteers.  Dictionaries, etc.
          .217                  Place names (General)
                                    For etymological studies, see PL8201, etc.
          .22                   Guidebooks
          .222                  General works
          .223                  General special
          .224                  Views
                                Historic monuments, landmarks, scenery, etc. (General)
                                    For local, see DT433.29
          .225                    General works
          .226                    Preservation
          .227                  Description and travel
          .23                   Antiquities
                                    For local antiquities, see DT433.29
          .24                   Social life and customs.  Civilization.  Intellectual
                                  life
                                    For specific periods, see the period or reign
                                Ethnography
          .242                    General works
          .245                    Individual elements in population, A-Z

                                    .B35   Bahima
                                    .B38   Bavuma
                                    .C55   Chiga
                                    .E18   East Indians
                                    .H38   Haya

                                    .I37   Ik
                                    .L3    Labwor

                                    .S24   Sapiny
                                    .S92   Sudanese
```

                  **Eastern Africa**
                    **East Africa.   British East Africa**
                      **Uganda** - Continued
                        **History**

| | |
|---|---|
| 433.252 | Biography (Collective) |
| |     For individual biography, <u>see</u> the specific |
| |         period or reign |
| .255 | Historiography |
| .257 | General works |
| .26 | Political history |
| |     For specific periods, <u>see</u> the period or reign |
| | Foreign and general relations |
| |     Class general works on the diplomatic history |
| |         of a period with the period, e. g. DT433.27+. |
| |     For works on relations with a specific |
| |         country regardless of period, <u>see</u> DT433.263 |
| .262 |   General works |
| .263 |   Relations with individual countries, A-Z |
| |     For list of countries, <u>see</u> pp. 212-214 |
| | **By period** |
| | Early to 1800 |
| .265 |   General works |
| |   Biography and memoirs |
| .266 |     Collective |
| .267 |     Individual, A-Z |
| | 1890-1962 |
| |     Including the Lugard Accords, activities of |
| |         the British East Africa Company, and |
| |         Buganda dominance |
| .27 |   General works |
| |   Biography and memoirs |
| .272 |     Collective |
| .273 |     Individual, A-Z |
| | 1962-1979.   Independent |
| .275 |   General works |
| |   Biography and memoirs |
| .279 |     Collective |
| .28 |     Individual, A-Z |
| .282 |   1962-1971 |
| .283 |   1971-1979.   Amin regime |
| |     Including Uganda-Tanzania War, 1978-1979 |

         **Eastern Africa**
           **East Africa.   British East Africa**
             **Uganda**
               **History**
                 **By period** - Continued
                   1979-

| | |
|---|---|
| 433.285 |              General works |
| |             Biography and memoirs |
| .286 |                 Collective |
| .287 |                 Individual, A-Z |
| .29 |        Local history and description, A-Z |

             **Kenya**
               For works on former British East Africa as a
                 whole, <u>see</u> DT421+

| | |
|---|---|
| .5 | Periodicals.   Societies.   Serials |
| .512 | Congresses |
| .513 | Sources and documents |
| .515 | Gazetteers.   Dictionaries, etc. |
| .517 | Place names (General) |
| |      For etymological studies, <u>see</u> PL8379, etc. |
| .52 | Guidebooks |
| .522 | General works |
| .523 | General special |
| .524 | Views |
| | Historic monuments, landmarks, scenery, etc. |
| |   (General) |
| |      For local, <u>see</u> DT434 |
| .525 |   General works |
| .526 |   Preservation |
| .527 | Description and travel |
| .53 | Antiquities |
| |      For local antiquities, <u>see</u> DT434 |
| .54 | Social life and customs.   Civilization. |
| |   Intellectual life |
| |      For specific periods, <u>see</u> the period or |
| |        reign |

              **Ethnography**

| | |
|---|---|
| .542 |   General works |
| .545 |   Individual elements in the population, A-Z |

                 .B67   Boran
                 .B74   British
                 .B84   Bukusu

                 .D54   Digo
                 .E27   East Indians

**Eastern Africa**
    **East Africa.   British East Africa**
      **Kenya**
      **Ethnography**

433.545          Individual elements in the population,
           A-Z - Continued

            .G32   Gabbra
            .G55   Giryama
            .G86   Gusii

            .I24   Ibibios

            .K36   Kamba
            .K55   Kikuyu
            .K57   Kipsigis
            .K87   Kuria
            .L63   Logooli *(handwritten)*
            .L85   Luo
            .L88   Luyia

            .M32   Marakwet
            .M33   Masai
            .M34   Mbere
            .M47   Meru

            .N34   Nandi
            .N55   Nika

            .P65   Pokomo

            .R45   Rendile

            .S83   Suba
            .S85   Suk

            .T34   Taita
            .T38   Taveta
            .T87   Turkana
            .T57   Tiriki *(handwritten)*

|          | Eastern Africa |
|----------|----------------|
|          | East Africa.   British East Africa |
|          | Kenya - Continued |
|          | History |
| 433.552  | Biography (Collective) |
|          | For individual biography, <u>see</u> the specific period, reign, or place |
| .555     | Historiography |
| .557     | General works |
|          | General special |
| .558     | General works |
| .559     | Political history |
|          | For specific periods, <u>see</u> the period or reign |
|          | Foreign and general relations |
|          | Class general works on the diplomatic history of a period with the period, e. g. DT433.565+.  For works on relations with a specific country regardless of period, <u>see</u> DT433.563 |
| .562     | General works |
| .563     | Relations with individual countries, A-Z |
|          | For list of countries, <u>see</u> pp. 212-214 |
|          | By period |
|          | Early to 1886.  Arab and Portuguese penetration. Coastal domination by the Sultanate of Zanzibar |
|          | Cf. DT449.Z2+, The Sultanate of Zanzibar |
| .565     | General works |
|          | Biography and memoirs |
| .566     | Collective |
| .567     | Individual, A-Z |
|          | 1886-1920.  Anglo-German accords on Zanzibar. Activities of the British East Africa Company in Kenya.  German claims to the Witu Protectorate.  East African Protectorate (1895-1920) |
|          | Cf. DT433.27, Activities of the British East Africa Company in general, and in Uganda |
| .57      | General works |
|          | Biography and memoirs |
| .572     | Collective |
| .573     | Individual, A-Z |

```
                    Eastern Africa
                      East Africa.   British East Africa
                        Kenya
                          History
                            By period - Continued
                              1920-1963.  Kenya Colony and Protectorate
        433.575                   General works
           .576                   Biography and memoirs
                                    .A2A-Z  Collective
                                    .A3-Z    Individual, A-Z
           .577                   Mau Mau move ment
                                  1963-
           .58                      General works
           .582                     Biography and memoirs
                                      .A2A-Z  Collective
                                      .A3-Z    Individual, A-Z
           .583                     1963-1978
           .584                     1978-
        434                     Local history and description, A-Z
                                  e. g.  Jubaland, see DT409.G58
        (435)                 Zanzibar, see DT449.Z2+
                      Tanzania.  Tanganyika.  German East Africa
                          Cf. DT450+, Rwanda.  Ruanda-Urundi
                          DT450.5+, Burundi
        436               Periodicals.  Societies.  Serials
                          Museums, exhibitions, etc.
           .2                General works
           .3                By place, A-Z
                                Subarranged by author
        437               Dictionaries.  Gazetteers, etc.
           .7             Guidebooks
        438             General works
                        Description and travel
        439               Early through 1918
        440               1919-1980
           .5             1981-
        442             Antiquities
           .5           Social life and customs.  Civilization.  Intellectual
                          life
                        Ethnography
        443               General works
           .3             Individual elements in the population, A-Z

                            .B37  Barabaig
                            .B65  Bondei
                            .F56  Fipa
                            .H67  Horombo
```

|  |  |  |
|---|---|---|

Eastern Africa
   Tanzania.   Tanganyika.   German East Africa
     Ethnography
443.3       Individual elements in the population,
           A-Z - Continued

       .K33  Kaguru
       .K47  Kerebe
       .K54  Kilindi
       .K87  Kuria

       .M34  Makonde
       .M37  Masai
       .M47  Meru
       .N43  Ndendeuli
       .N54  Ngoni
       .N58  Ngulu
       .N92  Nyakyusa
       .N93  Nyamwezi

       .P37  Pare

       .R35  Rangi
       .R64  Rogoro

       .S45  Shambala
       .S84  Suki
       .T32  Tabwa

       .W32  Wabena
       .W33  Wachaga
       .W36  Wapangwa
       .W39  Wazaramo
       .Z35  Zanaki

    **History**
.5      Biography (Collective)
       For individual biography, <u>see</u> the specific
         period, reign, or place
444      General works
      General special
445      Political history
       For specific periods, <u>see</u> the period
      Foreign and general relations
       Class general works on the diplomatic history
         of a period with the period, e. g. DT447+.
         For works on relations with a specific
         country regardless of period, <u>see</u> DT445.5
.3      General works
.5      Relations with individual countries, A-Z
       For list of countries, <u>see</u> pp. 212-214

```
                 Eastern Africa
                   Tanzania.  Tanganyika.  German East Africa
                     History - Continued
                       By period
                         Early and colonial
447                        General works
   .2                        Biography and memoirs
                               .A2A-Z  Collective
                               .A3-Z   Individual, A-Z
448                        Independent, 1961-1964
                           1964-     , United Republic of Tanzania
                               For Uganda-Tanzania War, 1978-1979,
                                 see DT433.283
   .2                        General works
   .25                       Biography and memoirs
                               .A2A-Z  Collective
                               .A3-Z   Individual, A-Z
449                        Regions, cities, etc., A-Z
                             e. g.  .I7      Iringa

                                    .K4      Kilimanjaro
                                    .K45     Kilwa Kisiwani Island

                                    .Z2-29  Zanzibar
                                    .Z2       Periodicals.  Societies.  Serials
                                    .Z22      Guidebooks
                                    .Z23      General works
                                    .Z24      Views
                                    .Z25      Description and travel
                                              History
                                    .Z26        General works
                                                By period
                                                  Early to 1890
                                    .Z27          General works
                                                  Biography and memoirs
                                    .Z273           Collective
                                    .Z274           Individual, A-Z
                                    .Z28        1890-1963
                                    .Z29        1963-
                                                For works about Zanzibar
                                                  and Tanganyika treated
                                                  together, see DT448.2
```

Eastern Africa - Continued
Rwanda.  Ruanda-Urundi
    Including works on Rwanda and Burundi together
    and works on Ruanda-Urundi.  For works on Burundi
    alone, see DT450.5+.  For works on German East
    Africa as a whole, see DT436+

| | |
|---|---|
| 450 | Periodicals.  Societies.  Serials |
| .115 | Gazetteers.  Dictionaries, etc. |
| .12 | Place names (General) |
| | For etymological studies, see PL8608, PL8611, etc. |
| .13 | Guidebooks |
| .14 | General works |
| .15 | General special |
| .16 | Views |
| | Historic monuments, landmarks, scenery, etc. (General) |
| | For local, see DT450.49 |
| .17 | General works |
| .18 | Preservation |
| .2 | Description and travel |
| .22 | Antiquities |
| | For local antiquities, see DT450.49 |
| .22 | Social life and customs.  Civilization.  Intellectual life |
| | For specific periods, see the period or reign |
| | Ethnography |
| .24 | General works |
| .25 | Individual elements in the population, A-Z |
| | **History** |
| .26 | Biography (Collective) |
| | For individual biography, see the specific period, reign, or place |
| .27 | Historiography |
| .28 | General works |
| | General special |
| .3 | Political history |
| | For specific periods, see the period or reign |
| | Foreign and general relations |
| | Class general works on the diplomatic history of a period with the period, e. g. DT450.34+.  For works on relations with a specific country regardless of period, see DT450.33 |
| .32 | General works |
| .33 | Relations with individual countries, A-Z |
| | For list of countries, see pp. 212-214 |

Eastern Africa
  Rwanda.  Ruanda-Urundi
   History - Continued
    **By period**
     Early to 1890.  Rwanda (Kingdom)

| | |
|---|---|
| 450.34 | General works |
| | Biography and memoirs |
| .35 | Collective |
| .36 | Individual, A-Z |

     1890-1916.  German domination

| | |
|---|---|
| .37 | General works |
| | Biography and memoirs |
| .38 | Collective |
| .39 | Individual, A-Z |

     1916-1945.  Belgian domination.  League of Nations mandate

| | |
|---|---|
| .4 | General works |
| | Biography and memoirs |
| .42 | Collective |
| .422 | Individual, A-Z |

     1945-1962.  United Nations mandate.  Belgian administration

| | |
|---|---|
| .425 | General works |
| | Biography and memoirs |
| .426 | Collective |
| .427 | Individual, A-Z |
| .43 | Civil War, 1959-1962 |
| .432 | Gitarama coup d'etat and dissolution of Rwanda-Tutsi monarchy, 1961 |

     1962-

| | |
|---|---|
| .435 | General works |
| | Biography and memoirs |
| .436 | Collective |
| .437 | Individual, A-Z |
| .49 | Local history and description, A-Z |

  **Burundi**

    For works on Rwanda and Burundi together, and for works on Ruanda-Urundi, <u>see</u> DT450+; for works on German East Africa as a whole, <u>see</u> DT436+

| | |
|---|---|
| .5 | Periodicals.  Societies.  Serials |
| .515 | Gazetteers.  Dictionaries, etc. |
| .52 | Place names (General) |
| | For etymological studies, <u>see</u> PL8608, PL8611, etc. |
| .53 | Guidebooks |
| .54 | General works |

**Eastern Africa**

**Burundi** - Continued

| | |
|---|---|
| 450.55 | General special |
| .56 | Views |
| | Historic monuments, landmarks, scenery, etc. (General) |
| |     For local, <u>see</u> DT450.95 |
| .57 |     General works |
| .58 |     Preservation |
| .6 | Description and travel |
| .62 | Antiquities |
| |     For local antiquities, <u>see</u> DT450.95 |
| .63 | Social life and customs. Civilization. Intellectual life |
| |     For specific periods, <u>see</u> the period or reign |
| | Ethnography |
| .64 |     General works |
| .65 |     Individual elements in the population, A-Z |

        .M67   Muslims

        .R86   Rundi

**History**

| | |
|---|---|
| .66 | Biography (Collective) |
| |     For individual biography, <u>see</u> the specific period, reign, or place |
| .67 | Historiography |
| .68 | General works |
| | General special |
| .7 |     Political history |
| |         For specific periods, <u>see</u> the period or reign |
| |     Foreign and general relations |
| |         Class general works on the diplomatic history of a period with the period, e. g. DT450.74+. For works on relations with a specific country regardless of period, <u>see</u> DT450.73 |
| .72 |     General works |
| .73 |     Relations with individual countries, A-Z |
| |         For list of countries, <u>see</u> pp. 212-214 |

Eastern Africa
  Burundi
    History - Continued
     By period
      Early to 1890.  Burundi (Kingdom)
450.74        General works
         Biography and memoirs
.75          Collective
.76          Individual, A-Z
      1890-1916.  German domination
.77        General works
         Biography and memoirs
.78          Collective
.79          Individual, A-Z

      1916-1945.  Belgian domination.  League of
        Nations mandate
.8        General works
         Biography and memoirs
.82          Collective
.83          Individual, A-Z

      1945-1962.  United Nations mandate.  Belgian
        administration
.84        General works
         Biography and memoirs
.842         Collective
.843         Individual, A-Z
      1962-
.85        General works
         Biography and memoirs
.852         Collective
.853         Individual, A-Z
.855       Dissolution of Burundi Tutsi monarchy, 1966

.95     Local history and description, A-Z

**Eastern Africa** - Continued
    **Islands (East African coast)**

| | |
|---|---|
| 468 | General works |
| | Ethnography |
| .42 | General works |
| .45 | Individual elements in the population, A-Z |

      .C45   Chinese

| | |
|---|---|
| 469 | Individual islands, A-Z |
| .A6 | Amirante Islands |
| .C7 | Comoro Islands |

      DT469.M497, Mayotte

**Madagascar**

| | |
|---|---|
| .M21 | Periodicals. Societies. Serials |
| .M22 | Sources and documents |
| .M24 | Gazetteers. Dictionaries, etc. |
| .M242 | Place names (General) |

      For etymological studies, <u>see</u> PL5371+, etc.

| | |
|---|---|
| .M25 | Guidebooks |
| .M26 | General works |
| .M262 | General special |
| .M265 | Views |

Historic monuments, landmarks, scenery, etc. (General)
    For local, <u>see</u> DT469.M37+

| | |
|---|---|
| .M266 | General works |
| .M267 | Preservation |
| .M273 | Antiquities |

    For local antiquities, <u>see</u> DT469.M37+

| | |
|---|---|
| .M274 | Social life and customs. Civilization. Intellectual life |

    For specific periods, <u>see</u> the period or reign
Ethnography

| | |
|---|---|
| .M276 | General works |
| .M277 | Individual elements in the population, A-Z |

      .M277A58   Antandroy
      .M277B37   Bara

      .M277H68   Hovas
      .M277M34   Mahafaly

```
              Eastern Africa
                Islands (East African coast)
      469             Individual islands, A-Z
                        Madagascar - Continued
                        Description and travel
                            To 1810, see DT469.M31+
                            1810-1900, see DT469.M32+
      .M28                    1901-
                        History
      .M282              Biography (Collective)
                            For individual biography, see the specific
                                period, reign, or place
                          Historiography
      .M283                General works
                            Biography of historians, area studies
                                specialists, archaeologists, etc.
      .M2835                Collective
      .M284                 Individual, A-Z
      .M285              General works
                          General special
      .M287                General works
      .M292                Political history
                            For specific periods, see the period
                                or reign
                          Foreign and general relations
                            Class general works on the diplomatic
                                history of a period with the period,
                                e. g. DT469.M31+.  For works on
                                relations with a specific country
                                regardless of period, see DT469.M297
      .M295                General works
      .M297                Relations with individual countries, A-Z
                            For list of countries, see pp. 212-214
                        By period
                          Early to 1810.  Early description and travel
      .M31                  General works
                            Biography and memoirs
      .M312                    Collective
      .M313                    Individual, A-Z
                          1810-1885.  19th century.  Hova rule
      .M32                   General works
                            Biography and memoirs
      .M321                    Collective
      .M322                    Individual, A-Z
```

```
                    Eastern Africa
                      Islands (East African coast)
        469               Individual islands, A-Z
                            Madagascar
                            History
                              By period
                                1810-1885.   19th century.   Hova
                                    rule - Continued
        .M323                         Radama I, 1810-1828
        .M324                         Ranavalona I (Ranavalo), 1828-1861
        .M326                         Radama II, 1861-1863
        .M328                         Rasoherina, 1863-1868
        .M33                          Ranavalona II (Ranavalo II),
                                          1868-1883
        .M335                         Ranavalona III (Ranavalo III),
                                          1883-1897
                                1885-1960.   French protectorate and
                                    colony
        .M34                          General works
                                      Biography and memoirs
        .M341                           Collective
        .M342                           Individual, A-Z
                                1960-     .  (Malagasy Republic)
        .M343                         General works
                                      Biography and memoirs
        .M344                           Collective
        .M345                           Individual, A-Z
                            Local history and description
        .M37                  Provinces, etc., A-Z

                              e. g.   .M37A52  Ambato-Boeni

                                      .M37A53  Androy

                                      .M37N67  Nossi-Be

        .M38                  Cities, towns, etc., A-Z

                                      Antananarivo, see .M38T34

                              .M38T33  Tamatave

                              .M38T34  Tananarive.  Antananarivo
```

Eastern Africa
  Islands (East African coast)

| | |
|---|---|
| 469 | Individual islands, A-Z - Continued |
| .M39 | Mascarene Islands |
| | **Mauritius (Ile de France)** |
| | Including Agalega, Rodrigues, and St. Brandon |
| .M4 | Periodicals.  Societies.   Serials |
| .M413 | Sources and documents |
| .M415 | Gazetteers.   Dictionaries, etc. |
| .M417 | Place names (General) |
| | For etymological studies, <u>see</u> PM7854, etc. |
| .M42 | Guidebooks |
| .M422 | General works |
| .M423 | General special |
| .M425 | Views |
| | Historic monuments, landmarks, scenery, etc. |
| | (General) |
| | For local, <u>see</u> DT469.M495 |
| .M426 | General works |
| .M427 | Preservation |
| .M429 | Description and travel |
| .M43 | Antiquities |
| | For local antiquities, <u>see</u> DT469.M491+ |
| .M44 | Social life and customs.  Civilization. |
| | Intellectual life |
| | For specific periods, <u>see</u> the period |
| | Ethnography |
| .M442 | General works |
| .M445 | Individual elements in the population, A-Z |
| | .M445B55  Blacks |
| | .M445E27  East Indians |
| | .M445T44  Telugus |
| | **History** |
| .M45 | Biography (Collective) |
| | For individual biography, <u>see</u> the specific |
| | period or place |
| .M452 | Historiography |

                          Eastern Africa
                            Islands (East African coast)
469                              Individual islands, A-Z
                                  Mauritius (Ile de France)
                                    History - Continued
                                      Study and teaching
.M453                                   General works
.M454                                    By region or country, A-Z
.M455                                  General works
                                       General special
.M457                                    Political history
                                           For specific periods, <u>see</u> the period
                                         Foreign and general relations
                                           Class works on the diplomatic history
                                             of a period with the period, e. g.
                                             DT469.M465+.  For works on relations
                                             with a specific country regardless of
                                             period, <u>see</u> DT469.M463
.M462                                      General works
.M463                                      Relations with individual countries, A-Z
                                             For list of countries, <u>see</u> pp. 212-214

                                     By period
                                       Early to 1810.  Dutch colonization.  French
                                           control.  Administration of the French
                                           East India Company
.M465                                      General works
                                           Biography and memoirs
.M466                                        Collective
.M467                                        Individual, A-Z
                                       1810-1968.  British domination
.M47                                       General works
                                           Biography and memoirs
.M472                                        Collective
.M473                                        Individual, A-Z
                                       1968-
.M48                                       General works
                                           Biography and memoirs
.M482                                        Collective
.M483                                        Individual, A-Z

**Eastern Africa**
  **Islands (East African coast)**
469         Individual islands, A-Z
          **Mauritius (Ile de France)** - Continued
            Local history and description
              Major islands and dependencies
.M491                 Agalega
                Chagos Archipelago, <u>see</u> DS349.9.C42
                Diego Garcia, <u>see</u> DS349.9.D53
.M492                 Rodrigues
.M493                 St. Brandon (Cargados Carajos)
.M495             Other local, A-Z
.M497           Mayotte
          Nossi-Be, <u>see</u> .M37N67

          **Réunion**
.R3             Periodicals. Societies. Serials
.R32            Gazetteers. Dictionaries, etc.
.R325          Guidebooks
.R33            General works
.R34            General special
.R345          Views
          Historic monuments, landmarks, scenery, etc.
            (General)
              For local, <u>see</u> DT469.R5
.R346          General works
.R347          Preservation
.R35            Description and travel
.R36            Antiquities
.R37            Social life and customs. Civilization.
            Intellectual life
              For specific periods, <u>see</u> the period
          Ethnography
.R38            General works
.R39            Individual elements in the population, A-Z

            .R39C48   Chinese

            .R39E28   East Indians

            .R39M87   Muslims

| | |
|---|---|
| | **Eastern Africa** |
| | **Islands (East African coast)** |
| 469 | Individual islands, A-Z |
| | **Réunion** - Continued |
| | **History** |
| .R42 | Biography (Collective) |
| | For individual biography, <u>see</u> the specific period, reign, or place |
| .R425 | Historiography |
| .R43 | General works |
| .R432 | Political history |
| | For specific periods, <u>see</u> the period |
| | Foreign and general relations |
| | For specific periods, <u>see</u> the period |
| .R435 | General works |
| .R436 | Relations with individual countries, A-Z |
| | For list of countries, <u>see</u> pp. 212-214 |
| | **By period** |
| | Early to 1764.   Compagnie des Indes Orientales |
| .R44 | General works |
| | Biography and memoirs |
| .R442 | Collective |
| .R443 | Individual, A-Z |
| | 1764-1946 |
| .R45 | General works |
| | Biography and memoirs |
| .R452 | Collective |
| .R453 | Individual, A-Z |
| | 1946- |
| .R455 | General works |
| | Biography and memoirs |
| .R457 | Collective |
| .R458 | Individual, A-Z |
| .R5 | Regions, cities, etc., A-Z |
| | |
| | **Seychelles** |
| .S4 | Periodicals.  Societies.  Serials |
| .S413 | Sources and documents |
| .S415 | Gazetteers.  Dictionaries, etc. |
| .S417 | Place names (General) |
| | For etymological studies, <u>see</u> PL8201, etc. |
| .S42 | Guidebooks |
| .S422 | General works |

|       |                                                      |
|-------|------------------------------------------------------|
|       | **Eastern Africa**                                   |
|       | **Islands (East African coast)**                     |
| 469   | Individual islands, A-Z                              |
|       | **Seychelles** - Continued                           |
| .S423 | General special                                      |
| .S424 | Views                                                |
|       | Historic monuments, landmarks, scenery, etc.         |
|       | (General)                                            |
|       | For local, <u>see</u> DT469.S49                      |
| .S425 | General works                                        |
| .S426 | Preservation                                         |
| .S427 | Description and travel                               |
| .S43  | Antiquities                                          |
|       | For local antiquities, <u>see</u> DT469.S49          |
| .S44  | Social life and customs.  Civilization.              |
|       | Intellectual life                                    |
|       | For specific periods, <u>see</u> the period or       |
|       | reign                                                |
|       | Ethnography                                          |
| .S442 | General works                                        |
| .S443 | Individual elements in the population, A-Z           |
|       |                                                      |
|       | **History**                                          |
| .S452 | Biography (Collective)                               |
|       | For individual biography, <u>see</u> the             |
|       | specific period, reign, or place                     |
| .S455 | Historiography                                       |
| .S457 | General works                                        |
|       | General special                                      |
| .S46  | Political history                                    |
|       | For specific periods, <u>see</u> the period          |
|       | or reign                                             |
|       | Foreign and general relations                        |
|       | Class general works on the diplomatic                |
|       | history of a period with the period,                 |
|       | e. g. DT469.S465+.  For works on                     |
|       | relations with a specific country                    |
|       | regardless of period, <u>see</u> DT469.S463          |
| .S462 | General works                                        |
| .S463 | Relations with individual countries, A-Z             |
|       | For list of countries, <u>see</u> pp. 212-214        |

Eastern Africa
  Islands (East African coast)
469        Individual islands, A-Z
                Seychelles
                  History - Continued
                    By period
                      Early to 1814.  Early explorations by Arabs,
                        Portuguese and British.  French colonial
                        rule.  British occupation between 1794-1814
  .S465                 General works
                        Biography and memoirs
  .S466                   Collective
  .S467                   Individual, A-Z
                      1814-1976.  British colonial rule
                        Including jurisdiction under Mauritius
                          from 1814-1903 and British Crown Colony
                          from 1903-1976
  .S47                  General works
                        Biography and memoirs
  .S472                   Collective
  .S473                   Individual, A-Z
                      1976
  .S48                  General works
                        Biography and memoirs
  .S482                   Collective
  .S483                   Individual, A-Z
  .S49            Local history and description, A-Z


## WEST AFRICA.  WEST COAST

470        Periodicals.  Societies.  Serials
  .2       Sources and documents
  .5       Guidebooks
471        General works
  .5       Views
472        Description and travel
473        Antiquities
                For local antiquities, see DT477+
474        Social life and customs.  Civilization.  Intellectual
             life
                For specific periods, see the period

|        | West Africa. West Coast - Continued |
|--------|-------------------------------------|
|        | Ethnography |
| 474.5  | General works |
| .6     | Individual elements in the population, A-Z |

|      |          |
|------|----------|
| .B73 | Brazilians |
| .C48 | Chamba |
| .E83 | Ewe |
| .F35 | Fang |
| .F84 | Fulahs |
| .G32 | Gbaya |
| .K78 | Kru |
| .M36 | Mandingo |
| .T46 | Tenda |
| .Y67 | Yorubas |

|        | **History** |
|--------|-------------|
| 475    | General works |
| .5     | Biography (Collective) |
|        | For individual biography, <u>see</u> the specific period, reign, or place |
|        | **By period** |
| 476    | Early to 1884 |
|        | 1884-1960. Colonial period |
| .2     | General works |
|        | Biography and memoirs |
| .22    | Collective |
| .23    | Individual, A-Z |
|        | 1960-   . Independent |
| .5     | General works |
|        | Biography and memoirs |
| .52    | Collective |
| .523   | Individual, A-Z |
|        | Local history and description, <u>see</u> DT477+ |

|  | West Africa.  West Coast - Continued |
|---|---|
| 477 | Upper Guinea |
| 479 | Lower Guinea |
|  | **British West Africa** |
| 491 | Periodicals.  Societies.  Serials |
| 493 | Dictionaries.  Guidebooks.  Directories |
| 494 | General works |
|  | Description and travel |
| 496 | Through 1800 |
| 497 | 1801-1950 |
| 498 | 1951- |
| 499 | Antiquities |
| 500 | Ethnography |
|  | **History** |
| 502 | General works |
| 503 | Other |
|  | Biography and memoirs |
| .9 | Collective |
| 504 | Individual, A-Z |
|  | **Local** |
| 507 | Ashanti Empire |
|  | Including works on the Ashantis and the Ashanti Wars |
|  | Cf. DT512.9.A84, Ashanti Region |
|  | Bornu, see DT515+ |
|  | **Gambia** |
|  | Cf. DT532.25, Senegambia |
| 509 | Periodicals.  Societies.  Serials |
| .13 | Sources and documents |
| .2 | Guidebooks |
| .22 | General works |
| .24 | Views |
| .27 | Description and travel |
| .4 | Social life and customs.  Civilization. Intellectual life |
|  | For specific periods, see the period |
|  | Ethnography |
| .42 | General works |
| .45 | Individual elements in the population, A-Z |
|  | .M34   Mandingo |
|  | .P67   Portuguese |
|  | .W64   Wolofs |

**West Africa. West Coast**
  **British West Africa**
    **Local**
      **Gambia** - Continued
        **History**

509.5         General works
         General special
          Foreign and general relations
           Class general works on the diplomatic history of a period with the period, e. g. DT509.65+. For works on relations with a specific country regardless of period, <u>see</u> DT509.63

 .62          General works
 .63          Relations with individual countries, A-Z
           For list of countries, <u>see</u> pp. 212-214
        **By period**
 .65         Early to 1894
 .7         1894-1965. British protectorate and colony
         1965- . Independent
 .8          General works
          Biography and memoirs
 .82           Collective
 .83           Individual, A-Z
 .9       Local history and description, A-Z

      **Ghana (Gold Coast)**
        Cf. DT532.15, Ghana empire
 .97        Periodicals. Societies. Serials
510         General works
 .15        Historic monuments, landmarks, scenery, etc. (General)
         For local, <u>see</u> DT512.9
 .2        Description and travel. Guidebooks
 .3        Antiquities
 .4        Social life and customs. Civilization. Intellectual life

West Africa.  West Coast
  British West Africa
    Local
      Ghana (Gold Coast) - Continued
        Ethnography

510.42          General works
  .43          Individual elements in the population, A-Z

      .A37  Afro-Americans
      .A53  Akans
            Ashantis, see DT507

      .B85  Builsa
      .D33  Dagari
      .D34  Dagomba

      .E94  Ewe
      .F35  Fantis

      .G3   Ga
      .G65  Gonja

      .K37  Kasena
      .K72  Krachi
      .K76  Krobo
      .K87  Kuranko
      .K93  Kwahu

      .M35  Mamprusi
      .N95  Nzima

      .S57  Sisala

      .T35  Talansi

        **History**
  .5          General works
  .6          Biography and memoirs (Collective)
            Political and diplomatic history.  Foreign
              and general relations.  Nationalism
  .62         General works
  .63         Relations with individual countries, A-Z
              For list of countries, see pp. 212-214

                    West Africa.  West Coast
                      British West Africa
                        Local
                          Ghana (Gold Coast)
                            History - Continued
                              By period
                                Early to 1957
                                    For Ashanti Empire, <u>see</u> DT507
511                                 General works
                                    Biography and memoirs
   .2                                   Collective
   .3                                   Individual, A-Z
                                Republic, 1957-
                                  1957-1979
512                                 General works
                                    Biography and memoirs
   .2                                     Collective
   .3                                     Individual, A-Z
                                  1979-
   .32                               General works
                                     Biography and memoirs
   .33                                   Collective
   .34                                   Individual, A-Z
   .9                            Local, A-Z


                              e. g.   .A84  Ashanti Region
                                            Cf. DT507, Ashanti Empire


(513)                         Yorubaland.  Yorubas, <u>see</u> DT474.6.Y67, West Africa;
                                DT515.45.Y67, Nigeria
                            **Nigeria**
515                           Periodicals.  Societies.  Serials
   .12                        Congresses
   .13                        Sources and documents
   .15                        Gazetteers.  Dictionaries, etc.
   .17                        Place names (General)
                                  For etymological studies, <u>see</u> PL8021.N5
   .2                         Guidebooks
   .22                        General works
   .23                        General special
   .24                        Views

        West Africa.  West Coast
          British West Africa
            Local
              Nigeria - Continued
                Historic monuments, landmarks, scenery, etc.
                  (General)
                    For local, <u>see</u> DT515.9

| | |
|---|---|
| 515.25 | General works |
| .26 | Preservation |
| .27 | Description and travel |
| .3 | Antiquities |

                    For local antiquities, <u>see</u> DT515.9

| | |
|---|---|
| .4 | Social life and customs.  Civilization. |
| | Intellectual life |

                    For specific periods, <u>see</u> the period
              Ethnography

| | |
|---|---|
| .42 | General works |
| .45 | Individual elements in the population, A-Z |

                    .A53  Angas

                    .B56  Bini
                    .B73  Brazilians

                    .D84  Dukawa

                    .E34  Efik
                    .E35  Egba
                    .F84  Fulahs

                    .G32  Gaanda
                    .G83  Gwari
                    .H38  Hausas

                    .I24  Ibibios
                    .I25  Idoma
                    .I32  Igala
                    .I33  Igbo
                    .I35  Ijo
                    .I86  Isoko

                          **West Africa.  West Coast**
                            **British West Africa**
                               **Local**
                                  **Nigeria**
                                      Ethnography

515.45                          Individual elements in the population,
                                    A-Z - Continued

                                 .J44   Jekri

                                 .K33   Kadara
                                 .K34   Kaleri
                                 .K36   Kanuri
                                 .K64   Kofyar
                                 .M33   Maguzawa
                                 .M35   Mambila
                                 .M62   Moba

                                 .N86   Nupe     .03  Ogba
                                 .O34   Ogori
                                 .O37   Okrika
                                 .R84   Rukuba

                                 .T58   Tivi
                                 .U24   Ubium

                                 .Y67   Yorubas

                             **History**
        .53                       Biography (Collective)
                               For individual biography, <u>see</u> the specific
                                   period, reign, or place
        .55                       Historiography
                               Study and teaching
        .556                    General works
        .557                    By region or country, A-Z
                                 Subarranged by author
        .57                       General works
        .58                       Juvenile works

           West Africa.  West Coast
             British West Africa
               Local
                 Nigeria
                   History - Continued
                     General special

| | |
|---|---|
| 515.585 | Military history |
| .59 | Political history |
| |    For specific periods, <u>see</u> the period |
| | Foreign and general relations |
| |    Class general works on the diplomatic |
| |      history of a period with the period, |
| |      e. g. DT515.65+.  For works on relations |
| |      with a specific country regardless of |
| |      period, <u>see</u> DT515.63 |
| .62 | General works |
| .63 | Relations with individual countries, A-Z |
| |    For list of countries, <u>see</u> pp. 212-214 |
| | **By period** |
| | Early to 1861 |
| .65 |    General works |
| |    Biography and memoirs |
| .66 |      Collective |
| .67 |      Individual, A-Z |
| | 1861-1914.  Period of colonization |
| .7 |    General works |
| |    Biography and memoirs |
| .72 |      Collective |
| .73 |      Individual, A-Z |
| | 1914-1960.  Colony and Protectorate of Nigeria |
| .75 |    General works |
| |    Biography and memoirs |
| .76 |      Collective |
| .77 |      Individual, A-Z |
| | 1960-    .   Independence |
| .8 |    General works |
| |    Biography and memoirs |
| .82 |      Collective |
| .83 |      Individual, A-Z |
| .832 |    1960-1966.  Balewa, Azikiwe and Ironsi |
| |    administrations |

West Africa.  West Coast
  British West Africa
   Local
    Nigeria
     History
      By period - Continued
       1966-1975.  Gowon administration
        Including January 1966 coup d'état

| | |
|---|---|
| 515.834 | General works |
| .836 | 1967-1970.  Civil war |
| |   Cf. DT515.9.E3, Eastern Region.  Biafra |
| .838 | 1975-1979.  Muhammad and Obasanjo administrations |
| |   Including 1975 coup d'état |
| .84  .842 | 1979-  — 1984 |
| .9 | Local history and description, A-Z |

         e. g.        Biafra, see .E3

            .E3  Eastern Region.  Biafra
               For Civil War, 1967-1970,
               see DT515.836

**Sierra Leone**

| | |
|---|---|
| 516 | Periodicals.  Societies.  Serials |
| .13 | Sources and documents |
| .15 | Gazetteers.  Dictionaries, etc. |
| .17 | Guidebooks |
| .18 | General works |
| .19 | Views |
| .2 | Description and travel |
| .4 | Social life and customs.  Civilization.  Intellectual life |
| |   For specific periods, see the period |
| | Ethnography |
| .42 | General works |
| .45 | Individual elements in the population, A-Z |

         .C73  Creoles

         .M45  Mende

         .T45  Temne

         .Y34  Yalunka

                    West Africa.  West Coast
                       British West Afric
                          Local
                             Sierra Leone - Continued
                                History
516.5                               General works
                                    General special
  .6                                   Political history
                                          For specific periods, <u>see</u> the period
                                       Foreign and general relations
                                          Class general works on the diplomatic
                                             history of a period with the period,
                                             e. g. DT516.65+.  For works on relations
                                             with a specific country regardless of
                                             period, <u>see</u> DT516.63
  .62                                     General works
  .63                                     Relations with individual countries, A-Z
                                             For list of countries, <u>see</u> pp. 212-214

                                 By period
  .65                                Early to 1787
                                     1787-1961.  British colony and protectorate
  .7                                    General works
                                        Biography and memoirs
  .719                                     Collective
  .72                                      Individual, A-Z
                                     1961-    .  Independent
  .8                                    General works
                                        Biography and memoirs
  .819                                     Collective
  .82                                      Individual, A-Z
  .9                               Local history and description, A-Z

                          e. g.   .F73  Freetown

|  | West Africa.  West Coast - Continued |
|---|---|
|  | French West Africa.  French Sahara.  West Sahara.  Sahel |
| 521 | Periodicals.  Societies.  Serials |
| 523 | Dictionaries.  Guidebooks.  Directories |
| 524 | General works |
| .5 | Views |
|  | Description and travel |
| 526 | Through 1800 |
| 527 | 1801-1950 |
| 528 | 1951- |
| 529 | Antiquities |
|  | Ethnography |
| 530 | General works |
| .5 | Individual elements in the population, A-Z |
|  | .B7    Brakna |
|  | .D64    Dogons |
|  | .F34    Fan |
|  | .F84    Fulahs |
|  | .J3    Jaawambe |
|  | .K64    Koniagui |
|  | .L42    Lebanese |
|  | .L43    Lebau |
|  | .M88    Muslims |
|  | .P94    Pygmies |
|  | .S65    Songhai |
|  | Tuaregs, _see_ DT346.T7 |
|  | **History** |
| 532 | General works |
|  | **Traditional kingdoms and empires** |
| .115 | Adamawa (Emirate) |
| .12 | Denkyira (Kingdom) |
| .13 | Futa-Jallon |
| .15 | Ghana empire |
|  | Cf. DT509.97+, Ghana |

West Africa.  West Coast
   French West Africa.  French Sahara.  West Sahara.  Sahel
      History
         **Traditional kingdoms and empires** - Continued

| | |
|---|---|
| 532.17 | Kaabu empire |
| .2 | Mali empire |
| |    Cf. DT551+, Mali Republic |
| .23 | Niumi (Kingdom) |
| .25 | Senegambia |
| |    Cf. DT509+, Gambia |
| |        DT549+, Senegal |
| .27 | Songhai empire |
| .3 | Toucouleur empire |
| .33 | Yatenga (Kingdom) |

*[handwritten annotation:] Foreign + gens rel. ... w/ period if about a per.*
*.39 General works*
*.395 Relations w/ ind. countries, A-Z*

         **By period**

| | |
|---|---|
| .4 | To 1884 |
| .5 | 1884-1960 |
| .6 | 1960- |
| | Biography and memoirs |
| 533.A2A-Z | Collective |
| .A3-Z | Individual, A-Z |

     **Local history and description**
      **Benin.  Dahomey**

| | |
|---|---|
| 541 | Periodicals.  Societies.  Serials |
| .13 | Sources and documents |
| .2 | Guidebooks |
| .22 | General works |
| .24 | Views |
| .27 | Description and travel |
| .4 | Social life and customs.  Civilization. |
| |   Intellectual life |
| |     For specific periods, <u>see</u> the period |
| | Ethnography |
| .42 |   General works |
| .45 |   Individual elements in the population, A-Z |
| |     .A33  Aja |
| |     .B37  Bariba |
| | |
| |     .F65  Fon |
| |     .G87  Gurma |
| | |
| |     .S65  Somba |
| |     .T63  Tofinnu |

           West Africa.   West Coast
             French West Africa.   French Sahara.   West Sahara.   Sahel
              Local history and description
               Benin.   Dahomey - Continued

|  |  |
|---|---|
|  | History |
| 541.5 | General works |
|  | General special |
|  | Foreign and general relations |
|  | Class general works on the diplomatic history of a period with the period, e. g. DT541.65+. For works on relations with a specific country regardless of period, <u>see</u> DT541.63 |
| .62 | General works |
| .63 | Relations with individual countries, A-Z |
|  | For list of countries, <u>see</u> pp. 212-214 |
|  |  |
|  | By period |
|  | Early to 1894 |
| .65 | General works |
|  | Biography and memoirs |
| .66 | Collective |
| .67 | Individual, A-Z |
| .75 | 1894-1960. French territory and colony |
|  | 1960-      Independent |
| .8 | General works |
|  | Biography and memoirs |
| .82 | Collective |
| .83 | Individual, A-Z |
| .84 | 1960-1972 |
|  | Including coups d'état by Soglo and Kouandete |
| .845 | 1972-      Kereko administration |
|  | Including 1972 coup d'état, 1975 name change from Dahomey to Benin, and 1977 coup attempt |
| .9 | Local history and description, A-Z |

West Africa.  West Coast
   French West Africa.  French Sahara.  West Sahara.  Sahel
     Local history and description - Continued
        Guinea

| | |
|---|---|
| 543 | Periodicals.  Societies.  Serials |
| .13 | Sources and documents |
| .2 | Guidebooks |
| .22 | General works |
| .24 | Views |
| .27 | Description and travel |
| .4 | Social life and customs.  Civilization.  Intellectual life |
| |    For specific periods, <u>see</u> the period |
| | Ethnography |
| .42 |   General works |
| .45 |   Individual elements in the population, A-Z |
| |     .F84  Fulahs |
| |     .M34  Mandingo |

**History**

| | |
|---|---|
| .5 | General works |
| | General special |
| .59 |   Political history |
| |   Foreign and general relations |
| |     Class general works on the diplomatic history of a period with the period, e. g. DT543.65+.  For works on relations with a specific country regardless of period, <u>see</u> DT543.63 |
| .62 |     General works |
| .63 |     Relations with individual countries, A-Z |
| |       For list of countries, <u>see</u> pp. 212-214 |

**By period**

| | |
|---|---|
| .65 | Early to 1895 |
| | 1895-1958.  French territory and colony |
| .75 |   General works |
| |   Biography and memoirs |
| .76 |     Collective |
| .77 |     Individual, A-Z |

West Africa.  West Coast
  French West Africa.  French Sahara.  West Sahara.  Sahel
   Local history and descrption
    Guinea
     History
      By period - Continued
       1958-   .  Independent

|  |  |
|---|---|
| 543.8 | General works |
|  | Biography and memoirs |
| .819 | Collective |
| .82 | Individual, A-Z |
|  | e. g.  .T68  Toure, Ahmed Sekou |
|  | 1958-1984 |
| .822 | General works |
|  | Biography and memoirs |
| .823 | Collective |
| .824 | Individual, A-Z |
|  | 1984- |
| .825 | General works |
|  | Biography and memoirs |
| .826 | Collective |
| .827 | Individual, A-Z |
| .9 | Local history and description, A-Z |
|  | **Ivory Coast** |
| 545 | Periodicals.  Societies.  Serials |
| .12 | Congresses |
| .13 | Sources and documents |
| .15 | Gazetteers.  Dictionaries, etc. |
| .17 | Place names (General) |
|  | For eytmological studies, <u>see</u> PL8021.I8 |
| .2 | Guidebooks |
| .22 | General works |
| .23 | General special |
| .24 | Views |
| .27 | Description and travel |
| .3 | Antiquities |
|  | For local antiquities, <u>see</u> DT545.9 |
| .4 | Social life and customs.  Civilization. |
|  | Intellectual life |
|  | For specific periods, <u>see</u> the period |

West Africa.  West Coast
   French West Africa.  French Sahara.  West Sahara.  Sahel
     Local history and description
      Ivory Coast - Continued
       Ethnography

| | |
|---|---|
| 545.42 | General works |
| .45 | Individual elements in the population, A-Z |

|  |  |
|---|---|
| .A27 | Abron |
| | Agni, see .A58 |
| .A58 | Anyi |
| .B36 | Baoule |
| .B47 | Bété |
| .D85 | Dyula |
| .G33 | Gade |
| .G34 | Gagou |
| .G47 | Gere |
| .G87 | Guro |
| .K77 | Kru |
| .O96 | Ouobe |
| .S44 | Senufo |
| .V47 | Vere |

**History**

| | |
|---|---|
| .52 | Biography (Collective) |
| |   For individual biography, see the specific period, reign, or place |
| .55 | Historiography |
| .57 | General works |
| .58 | Juvenile works |
| | General special |
| .59 | Political history   *For specific periods, see per* |
| | Foreign and general relations |
| |   Class general works on the diplomatic history of a period with the period, e. g. DT545.7+.  For works on relations with a specific country regardless of period, see DT545.63 |
| .62 | General works |
| .63 | Relations with individual countries, A-Z |
| |   For list of countries, see pp. 212-214 |

West Africa.  West Coast
  French West Africa.  French Sahara.  West Sahara.  Sahel
    Local history and description
      Ivory Coast
        History - Continued
          By period
            Early to 1893

|         |                                          |
|---------|------------------------------------------|
| 545.7   | General works                            |
|         | Biography and memoirs                    |
| .72     | Collective                               |
| .73     | Individual, A-Z                          |
|         | 1893-1960                                |
| .75     | General works                            |
|         | Biography and memoirs                    |
| .76     | Collective                               |
| .77     | Individual, A-Z                          |
|         | 1960-    .  Independence                 |
| .8      | General works                            |
|         | Biography and memoirs                    |
| .82     | Collective                               |
| .83     | Individual, A-Z                          |
| .9      | Local history and description, A-Z       |

  **French-speaking Equatorial Africa**
    **Gabon (Gaboon, Gabun)**

|          |                                          |
|----------|------------------------------------------|
| 546.1    | Periodicals.  Societies.  Serials        |
| .113     | Sources and documents                    |
| .115     | Gazetteers.  Dictionaries, etc.          |
| .12      | Guidebooks                               |
| .122     | General works                            |
| .124     | Views                                    |
|          |                                          |
|          | Description and travel                   |
| .127     | Through 1980                             |
| .128     | 1981-                                    |
| .14      | Social life and customs.  Civilization.  |
|          | Intellectual life                        |
|          | For specific periods, <u>see</u> the period |

West Africa.  West Coast
  French West Africa.  French Sahara.  West Sahara.  Sahel
    Local history and description
     French-speaking Equatorial Africa
      Gabon (Gaboon, Gabun) - Continued
       Ethnography

| | |
|---|---|
| 546.142 |   General works |
| .145 |   Individual elements in the population, A-Z |

     .B35 Bantu-speakr

     .F34  Fang
     .G34  Galwa

     .M66  Mpongwe
     .M93  Myene

     .N56  Nkomi
     .N93  Nzabi

**History**

| | |
|---|---|
| .15 | General works |
| | General special |
| |   Foreign and general relations |
| |     Class general works on the diplomatic history of a period with the period, e. g. DT546.165+.  For works on relations with a specific country regardless of period, <u>see</u> DT546.163 |
| .162 |     General works |
| .163 |     Relations with individual countries, A-Z |
| |       For list of countries, <u>see</u> pp. 212-214 |
| | **By period** |
| .165 | Early to 1886 |
| .175 | 1886-1960.  French colony and territory |
| | 1960-   .  Independent |
| .18 |   General works |
| |   Biography and memoirs |
| .182 |     Collective |
| .183 |     Individual, A-Z |
| .19 | Local history and description, A-Z |

    e. g.  .L5  Libreville

West Africa.  West Coast
    French West Africa.  French Sahara.  West Sahara.  Sahel
      Local history and description
        French-speaking Equatorial Africa - Continued
          Congo (Brazzaville).  Middle Congo

| | |
|---|---|
| 546.2 | Periodicals.  Societies.  Serials |
| .213 | Sources and documents |
| .215 | Gazetteers.  Dictionaries, etc. |
| .22 | Guidebooks |
| .223 | General works |
| .234 | Views |
| .227 | Description and travel |
| .24 | Social life and customs.  Civilization. |
| |   Intellectual life |
| |     For specific periods, <u>see</u> the period |
| | Ethnography |
| .242 |   General works |
| .245 |   Individual elements in the population, A-Z |

          .B44  Bembe

          .N86  Nunu

          .T43  Teke

| | |
|---|---|
| | **History** |
| .25 | General works |
| | General special |
| |   Foreign and general relations |
| |     Class general works on the diplomatic |
| |     history of a period with the period, |
| |     e. g. DT546.256+.  For works on |
| |     relations with a specific country |
| |     regardless of period, <u>see</u> DT546.263 |
| .262 |   General works |
| .263 |   Relations with individual countries, A-Z |
| |     For list of countries, <u>see</u> pp. 212-214 |
| | **By period** |
| | Early to 1910 |
| .265 |   General works |
| |   Biography and memoirs |
| .266 |     Collective |
| .267 |     Individual, A-Z |

          e. g.  .B72  Brazza, Pierre
                        Savorgnan de,
                        1852-1905

West Africa.   West Coast
   French West Africa.   French Sahara.   West Sahara.   Sahel
    Local history and description
     French-speaking Equatorial Africa
      Congo (Brazzaville).   Middle Congo
       History
        By period - Continued

|          |                                                      |
|----------|------------------------------------------------------|
| 546.275  | 1910-1960.   French colony and territory             |
|          | 1960-       .   Independent                          |
| .28      | General works                                        |
|          | Biography and memoirs                                |
| .282     | Collective                                           |
| .283     | Individual, A-Z                                      |
| .29      | Local history and description, A-Z                   |

Central African Republic.   Central African Empire.
   Ubangi-Shari

|          |                                                      |
|----------|------------------------------------------------------|
| .3       | Periodicals.   Societies.   Serials                  |
| .313     | Sources and documents                                |
| .315     | Gazetteers                                           |
| .32      | Guidebooks                                           |
| .322     | General works                                        |
| .324     | Views                                                |
| .327     | Description and travel                               |
| .33      | Antiquities                                          |
|          | For local antiquities, see DT546.39                  |
| .34      | Social life and customs.   Civilization.             |
|          | Intellectual life                                    |
|          | For specific periods, see the period                 |
|          | Ethnography                                          |
| .342     | General works                                        |
| .345     | Individual elements in the population, A-Z           |

        .A35   Aka

        .B33   Babingas

        .M38   Mbum

        .N44   Ngbaka (Lobaye)

       West Africa.   West Coast
        French West Africa.  French Sahara.  West Sahara.  Sahel
         Local history and description
          French-speaking Equatorial Africa
           Central African Republic.  Central African Empire.
            Ubangi-Shari - Continued
            **History**

| | |
|---|---|
| 546.348 | Historiography |
| .35 | General works |
| | General special |
| | Foreign and general relations |
| |   Class general works on the diplomatic history of a period with the period, e. g. DT546.365+.  For works on relations with a specific country regardless of period, <u>see</u> DT546.363 |
| .362 | General works |
| .363 | Relations with individual countries, A-Z <br>   For list of countries, <u>see</u> pp. 212-214 |

| | |
|---|---|
| | **By period** |
| .365 | Early to 1910 |
| .37 | 1910-1960.  French colony |
| | 1960-    .  Independent |
| .375 | General works |
| | 1960-1979 <br>   Including Central African Empire, 1976-1979 |
| .38 | General works |
| | Biography and memoirs |
| .382 | Collective |
| .383 | Individual, A-Z |

               e. g.   .B64   Bokassa I

| | |
|---|---|
| <del>.384</del> | 1979- |
| .39 | Local history and description, A-Z |

*[handwritten annotations:]*

.384         General works

.385         Biography + memoirs

.3852        Collective

               Individual, A-Z

                  e.g. .K6 Kolingba, André

West Africa.  West Coast
  French West Africa.  French Sahara.  West Sahara.  Sahel
    Local history and description
      French-speaking Equatorial Africa - Continued
        Chad (Tchad)

| | |
|---|---|
| 546.4 | Periodicals.  Societies.  Serials |
| .413 | Sources and documents |
| .42 | Guidebooks |
| .422 | General works |
| .424 | Views |
| .427 | Description and travel |
| .43 | Antiquities |
| |     For local antiquities, see DT546.49 |
| .44 | Social life and customs.  Civilization. |
| |   Intellectual life |
| |     For specific periods, see the period |
| | Ethnography |
| .442 |   General works |
| .445 |   Individual elements in the population, A-Z |

        .B34  Bagirmi

        .K36  Kanembu

        .M37  Masa

        .M85  Mundang

        .N35  Nar

        .S25  Sao
        .S27  Sara
        .T43  Teda

**History**

| | |
|---|---|
| .457 |   General works |
| |   General special |
| .46 |     Political history |
| |       For specific periods, see the period |

West Africa. West Coast
  French West Africa. French Sahara. West Sahara. Sahel
    Local history and description
      French-speaking Equatorial Africa
        Chad (Tchad)
          History
             General special - Continued
                Foreign and general relations
                    Class general works on the diplomatic
                      history of a period with the period,
                      e. g. DT546.47+. For works on
                      relations with a specific country
                      regardless of period, see DT546.463

| | |
|---|---|
| 546.462 | General works |
| .463 | Relations with individual countries, A-Z |
| |   For list of countries, see pp. 212-214 |
| | **By period** |
| | Early to 1910 |
| .47 | General works |
| | Biography and memoirs |
| .472 | Collective |
| .473 | Individual, A-Z |
| | 1910-1960 |
| .475 | General works |
| | Biography and memoirs |
| .476 | Collective |
| .477 | Individual, A-Z |
| | 1960-    . Independent |
| .48 | General works |
| | Biography and memoirs |
| .482 | Collective |
| .483 | Individual, A-Z |
| .49 | Local history and description, A-Z |

        e. g.   .L34  Lake Chad

             .W33  Wadai

**West Africa. West Coast**
  **French West Africa. French Sahara. West Sahara. Sahel**
    **Local history and description** - Continued
      **Niger**

| | |
|---|---|
| 547 | Periodicals. Societies. Serials |
| .13 | Sources and documents |
| .2 | Guidebooks |
| .22 | General works |
| .24 | Views |
| .27 | Description and travel |
| .4 | Social life and customs. Civilization. Intellectual life |
| |   For specific periods, <u>see</u> the period |
| | Ethnography |
| .42 |   General works |
| .45 |   Individual elements in the population, A-Z |

           .B67   Bororo

           .F84   Fulahs
           .H38   Hausas

           .M38   Mawri

           .S65   Songhai

           .T83   Tuaregs

           .Z37   Zarma

      **History**

| | |
|---|---|
| .5 | General works |
| | General special |
| | Foreign and general relations |
| |   Class general works on the diplomatic history of a period with the period, e. g. DT547.65+. For works on relations with a specific country regardless of period, <u>see</u> DT547.63 |
| .62 | General works |
| .63 | Relations with individual countries, A-Z |
| |   For list of countries, <u>see</u> pp. 212-214 |

                        West Africa.  West Coast
                          French West Africa.  French Sahara.  West Sahara.  Sahel
                            Local history and description
                              Niger
                                History - Continued
                                  By period
547.65                               Early to 1900
   .75                                 1900-1960.  French territory and colony
                                       1960-   .  Independent
   .8                                    General works
                                         Biography and memoirs
   .82                                      Collective
   .83                                      Individual, A-Z
   .9                                Local history and description, A-Z

                                     e. g.   .N5   Niamey

                                        Niger River, see DT360


548                           West Sahara

                            Senegal
549                           Periodicals.  Societies.  Serials
   .12                          Congresses
   .13                          Sources and documents
   .15                          Gazetteers.  Dictionaries, etc.
   .17                          Place names (General)
                                  For etymological studies, see PL8021.S4
   .2                           Guidebooks
   .22                          General works
   .23                          General special
   .24                          Views
   .27                          Description and travel
   .3                           Antiquities
                                  For local antiquities, see DT549.9
   .4                           Social life and customs.  Civilization.
                                  Intellectual life
                                    For specific periods, see the period

|  |  |
|---|---|
|  | West Africa.  West Coast |
|  | French West Africa.  French Sahara.  West Sahara.  Sahel |
|  | Local history and description |
|  | Senegal - Continued |
|  | Ethnography |
| 549.42 | General works |
| .45 | Individual elements in the population, A-Z |

         .B35  Banjal

         .B37  Bassari

         .B39  Bayot

         .F84  Fulahs

         .L42  Lebou

         .S47  Serers

         .S66  Soninke

         .T68  Toucouleurs

         .W64  Wolofs

|  |  |
|---|---|
|  | **History** |
| .47 | Biography (Collective) |
|  | For individual biography, <u>see</u> the specific period or place |
| .48 | Historiography |
| .5 | General works |
| .52 | Juvenile works |
|  | General special |
| .59 | Political history |
|  | For specific periods, <u>see</u> the period |
|  | Foreign and general relations |
|  | Class general works on the diplomatic history of a period with the period, e. g. DT549.7+.  For works on relations with a specific country regardless of period, <u>see</u> DT549.63 |
| .62 | General works |
| .63 | Relations with individual countries, A-Z |
|  | For list of countries, <u>see</u> pp. 212-214 |

West Africa.  West Coast
  French West Africa.  French Sahara.  West Sahara.  Sahel
    Local history and description
      Senegal
        History - Continued
          By period
            Early to 1895
              Cf. DT532.25, Senegambia

549.7                  General works
              Biography and memoirs
.72                 Collective
.73                 Individual, A-Z
            1895-1960
              Cf. DT551.8+, Mali (Federation)
.75                General works
              Biography and memoirs
.76                 Collective
.77                 Individual, A-Z
            1960-   .  Independent
              Cf. DT551.8+, Mali (Federation)
.8                 General works
              Biography and memoirs
.82                 Collective
.83                 Individual, A-Z
.9          Local history and description, A-Z

      **Mali.  Mali Federation.  Soudanese Republic.**
        **French Sudan**
         Cf. DT532.2, Mali empire
551         Periodicals.  Societies.  Serials
.13        Sources and documents
.15        Gazetteers.  Dictionaries, etc.
.2        Guidebooks
.22        General works
.24        Views
.27        Description and travel
.3        Antiquities
         For local antiquities, <u>see</u> DT551.9

*Historic monuments, landmarks, scenery, etc (General)*
*For local, <u>see</u>  DT551.9*
*General works*
*Preservations*

.25
.26

        West Africa.  West Coast
          French West Africa.  French Sahara.  West Sahara.  Sahel
            Local history and description
              Mali.  Mali Federation.  Soudanese Republic.
                French Sudan - Continued

551.4             Social life and customs.  Civilization.
                Intellectual life
                    For specific periods, see the period
              Ethnography
  .42               General works
  .45               Individual elements in the population, A-Z

                  .B35   Bambara

                  .D45   Dendi

                  .D64   Dogons

                  .F85   Fulahs

                  .M36   Mandingo

            **History**
  .5               General works
              General special
  .6                 Political history
                    For specific periods, see the period
                Foreign and general relations
                    Class general works on the diplomatic
                      history of a period with the period,
                      e. g. DT551.65+.  For works on
                      relations with a specific country
                      regardless of period, see DT551.63
  .62              General works
  .63              Relations with individual countries, A-Z
                    For list of countries, see pp. 212-214

West Africa. West Coast
  French West Africa. French Sahara. West Sahara. Sahel
    Local history and description
      Mali. Mali Federation. Soudanese Republic.
        French Sudan
        History - Continued
          By period

| | |
|---|---|
| 551.65 |       Early to 1898 |
| |       1898-1959. French colony and territory |
| .7 |         General works |
| |         Biography and memoirs |
| .719 |           Collective |
| .72 |           Individual, A-Z |
| |       1959- |
| |         Including Mali Federation (April 1959- |
| |           Aug. 1960) and Mali Republic, (1960-     ) |
| |         Cf. DT549.75+, Senegal |
| .8 |         General works |
| |         Biography and memoirs |
| .819 |           Collective |
| .82 |           Individual, A-Z |
| |           e. g.  .K44  Keita, Modibo |
| .9 |       Local history and description, A-Z |
| |         e. g.  .T55  Timbuktu |

**Mauritania**

| | |
|---|---|
| 554 |       Periodicals. Societies. Serials |
| .13 |       Sources and documents |
| .15 |       Gazetteers. Dictionaries, etc. |
| .17 |       Place names (General) |
| |         For etymological studies, <u>see</u> PL8181+ |
| .2 |       Guidebooks |
| .22 |       General works |
| .23 |       General special |
| .24 |       Views |
| |       Historic monuments, landmarks, scenery, etc. |
| |         (General) |
| |         For local, <u>see</u> DT554.9 |
| .25 |         General works |
| .26 |         Preservation |

West Africa.  West Coast
  French West Africa.  French Sahara.  West Sahara.  Sahel
    Local history and description
      Mauritania - Continued

| | |
|---|---|
| 554.27 | Description and travel |
| .3 | Antiquities |
| |   For local antiquities, <u>see</u> DT554.9 |
| .4 | Social life and customs.  Civilization. Intellectual life |
| |   For specific periods, <u>see</u> the period or reign |
| | Ethnography |
| .42 |   General works |
| .45 |   Individual elements in the population, A-Z |

        .M84  Muslims
        .S65  Soninke

**History**

| | |
|---|---|
| .52 | Biography (Collective) |
| |   For individual biography, <u>see</u> the specific period, reign, or place |
| .55 | Historiography |
| .57 | General works |
| | General special |
| .58 |   General works |
| .59 |   Political history |
| |     For specific periods, <u>see</u> the period or reign |
| | Foreign and general relations |
| |   Class general works on the diplomatic history of a period with the period, e. g. DT554.65+.  For works on relations with a specific country regardless of period, <u>see</u> DT554.63 |
| .62 | General works |
| .63 | Relations with individual countries, A-Z |
| |   For list of countries, <u>see</u> pp. 212-214 |

West Africa.  West Coast
  French West Africa.  French Sahara.  West Sahara.  Sahel
    Local history and description
      Mauritania
        History - Continued
          By period
            Early to 1920.  Arab and Berber Almoravid
              domination.  Early explorations by
              Portuguese, English and French.  Early
              colonization by French, including
              negotiations by Xavier Coppolani
                Cf. DT318+, Morocco
                    DT532+, French West Africa
                    DT532.15, Ghana empire

| | |
|---|---|
| 554.65 | General works |
| | Biography and memoirs |
| .66 |   Collective |
| .67 |   Individual, A-Z |
| | 1920-1960.  French colony |
| .75 | General works |
| | Biography and memoirs |
| .76 |   Collective |
| .77 |   Individual, A-Z |
| | 1960-    .  Independent |
| |   Including Moroccan annexation claims |
| |   Cf. DT346.S7, Spanish Sahara |
| .8 | General works |
| | Biography and memoirs |
| .82 |   Collective |
| .83 |   Individual, A-Z |
| .9 | Local history and description, A-Z |

West Africa.  West Coast
French West Africa.  French Sahara.  West Sahara.  Sahel
Local history and description - Continued
Burkina Faso.  Upper Volta

| | |
|---|---|
| 555 | Periodicals.  Societies.  Serials |
| .13 | Sources and documents |
| .15 | Gazetteers.  Dictionaries, etc. |
| .17 | Place names (General) |
| | For etymological studies, <u>see</u> PL8521+ |
| .2 | Guidebooks |
| .22 | General works |
| .23 | General special |
| .24 | Views |
| | Historic monuments, landmarks, scenery, etc. (General) |
| | For local, <u>see</u> DT555.9 |
| .25 | General works |
| .26 | Preservation |
| .27 | Description and travel |
| .3 | Antiquities |
| | For local antiquities, <u>see</u> DT555.9 |
| .4 | Social life and customs.  Civilization.  Intellectual life |
| | For specific periods, <u>see</u> the period or reign |
| | Ethnography |
| .42 | General works |
| .45 | Individual elements in the population, A-Z |

.B57  Bisa
.B63  Bobo
.B64  Bobo Dioula
.D35  Dagari

.F85  Fulahs
.G85  Gurma
.G87  Gurunsi

.K88  Kurumba
.L63  Lobi
.L68  LoWilli

.M67  Mossi

.T87  Tusia

**West Africa.  West Coast**
   **French West Africa.  French Sahara.  West Sahara.  Sahel**
      **Local history and description**
         **Burkina Faso.  Upper Volta** - Continued
            **History**

|         |                              |
|---------|------------------------------|
| 555.52  | Biography (Collective)       |

                For individual biography, <u>see</u> the specific
                   period, reign, or place

| .55 | Historiography |
| .57 | General works |
|     | General special |
| .59 | Political history |

                For specific periods, <u>see</u> the period or
                   reign

            Foreign and general relations
               Class general works on the diplomatic
                 history of a period with the period,
                 e. g. DT555.65+.  For works on relations
                 with a specific country regardless of
                 period, <u>see</u> DT555.63

| .62 | General works |
| .63 | Relations with individual countries, A-Z |

                For list of countries, <u>see</u> pp. 212-214

           **By period**
             Early to 1897.  Mossi and Gourma Kingdoms.
             Moroccan conquest.  Early European
             explorations.  Invasions by Samory
               Cf. DT319, Morocco, 647-1516

| .65 | General works |
|     | Biography and memoirs |
| .66 | Collective |
| .67 | Individual, A-Z |

West Africa.  West Coast
  French West Africa.  French Sahara.  West Sahara.  Sahel
   Local history and description
    Burkina Faso.  Upper Volta
     History
      By period - Continued
       1897-1960.  French Protectorate and Colony
        Including administration as part of Upper
         Senegal-Niger (1904-1919)
         Cf. DT545, Ivory Coast (Partition during
          years 1932-1947)
          DT547, Niger (Partition during years
          1932-1947)
          DT551, French Sudan (Mali) (Partition
          during years 1932-1947)

| | |
|---|---|
| 555.75 | General works |
| | Biography and memoirs |
| .76 | Collective |
| .77 | Individual, A-Z |
| | 1960- |
| .8 | General works |
| | Biography and memoirs |
| .82 | Collective |
| .83 | Individual, A-Z |
| .9 | Local history and description, A-Z |

**Cameroon (Cameroun, Kamerun)**
  Formerly German West Africa

| | |
|---|---|
| 561 | Periodicals.  Societies.  Serials |
| 562 | Sources and documents |
| 563 | Gazetteers.  Dictionaries, etc. |
| .5 | Guidebooks |
| 564 | General works |
| | Description and travel |
| 566 | Through 1918 |
| 567 | 1919-1980 |
| 568 | 1981- |
| 569 | Antiquities |
| | For local antiquities, see DT581 |
| .5 | Social life and customs.  Civilization.  Intellectual life |
| | For specific periods, see the period |

West Africa.  West Coast
  Cameroon (Cameroun, Kamerun) - Continued
    Ethnography
570         General works
571         Individual elements in the population, A-Z

| | |
|---|---|
| .B3 | Babingas |
| .B32 | Bafia |
| .B323 | Bakwiri |
| .B33 | Bali |
| .B34 | Bamileke |
| .B35 | Bamun |
| .B36 | Bana |
| .B37 | Basa |
| .B38 | Bavëk |
| .B47 | Beti |
| .B67 | Bororo |
| .D68 | Dowayo |
| .D83 | Duala |
| .E86 | Eton |
| .E94 | Evuzok |
| .F64 | Fon |
| .F43 | Fe'Fe |
| .F73 | French |
| .F84 | Fula |
| .K66 | Kossi |
| .M35 | Maka |
| .P93 | Pygmies |

<pre>
                    West Africa.  West Coast
                      Cameroon (Cameroun, Kamerun) - Continued
                        History
        572                 General works
                            General special
                              Foreign and general relations
                                Class general works on the diplomatic history
                                  of a period with the period, e. g. DT574+.
                                  For works on relations with a specific
                                  country regardless of period, see DT573.5
        573                     Sources and documents
          .3                    General works
          .5                    Relations with individual countries, A-Z
                                    For list of countries, see pp. 212-214
                        By period
                          Early to 1960
        574                   General works
                              Biography and memoirs
          .5                    Collective
        575                     Individual, A-Z

                                    e. g.   .D6  Dominik, Hans

                              1960-     .  Republic
          .5                    General works
                                1960-1982.  Ahidjo administration
        576                       General works
                                  Biography and memoirs
          .5                        Collective
        577                         Individual, A-Z
                                1982-
        578                       General works
                                  Biography and memoirs
          .3                        Collective
          .4                        Individual, A-Z
        581                 Local history and description, A-Z
</pre>

West Africa.  West Coast
Togo.  Togoland

| | |
|---|---|
| 582 | Periodicals.  Societies.  Serials |
| .13 | Sources and documents |
| .15 | Gazetteers.  Dictionaries, etc. |
| .2 | Guidebooks |
| .22 | General works |
| .24 | Views |
| .27 | Description and travel |
| .4 | Social life and customs.  Civilization.  Intellectual life |

For specific periods, see the period

Ethnography

| | |
|---|---|
| .42 | General works |
| .45 | Individual elements in the population, A-Z |

.A34  Aja

.K33  Kabre

.M55  Mina

**History**

| | |
|---|---|
| .5 | General works |
| | General special |
| .59 | Political history |

For specific periods, see the period

Foreign and general relations
Class general works on the diplomatic history
of a period with the period, e. g. DT582.65+.
For works on relations with a specific
country regardless of period, see DT582.63

| | |
|---|---|
| .62 | General works |
| .63 | Relations with individual countries, A-Z |

For list of countries, see pp. 212-214

**By period**

| | |
|---|---|
| .65 | To 1884 |
| .7 | 1884-1922.  German colony |
| | 1922-1960.  Partition |
| .75 | French Togoland (1922-1960) |
| | British Togoland (1922-1957), see DT511+ |

                    West Africa.  West Coast
                      Togo.  Togoland
                        History
                          By period - Continued
                            1960-    .  Independent
582.8                          General works
                                 Biography and memoirs
    .819                           Collective
    .82                            Individual, A-Z

                                   e. g.   .E94  Eyadema, Gnassingbe

    .9                 Local history and description, A-Z

                                   e. g.   .L65  Lome

                    **Portuguese-speaking West Africa**
591                   Periodicals.  Societies.  Serials
593                   Guidebooks
594                   General works
                      Description and travel
596                     Through 1800
597                     1801-1950
598                     1951-
599                   Antiquities
600                   Ethnography
602                   History
                    **Local history and description**
                      Cape Verde Islands, <u>see</u> DT671.C2+
                      **Guinea-Bissau.   Portuguese Guinea**
613                     Periodicals.  Societies.  Serials
    .13                   Sources and documents
    .16                   Guidebooks
    .17                   General works
    .19                   Views
    .2                    Description and travel
    .4                    Social life and customs.  Civilization.
                            Intellectual life
                              For specific periods, <u>see</u> the period

```
                West Africa.  West Coast
                  Portuguese-speaking West Africa
                    Local history and description
                      Guinea-Bissau.  Portuguese Guinea - Continued
                            Ethnography
613.42                        General works
    .45                       Individual elements in the population, A-Z

                        .M36  Mandingo

                      History
    .5                    General works
                          General special
    .6                      Political history
                                For specific periods, see the period
                            Foreign and general relations
                                Class general works on the diplomatic
                                  history of a period with the period,
                                  e. g. DT613.65+.  For works on relations
                                  with a specific country regardless of
                                  period, see DT613.63
    .62                         General works
    .63                         Relations with individual countries, A-Z
                                  For list of countries, see pp. 212-214
                          By period
    .65                     Early to 1879
                            1879-1974.  Portuguese colony and territory
    .75                       General works
                              Biography and memoirs
    .752                         Collective
    .76                          Individual, A-Z

                              e. g.  .C3  Cabral, Amilcar

    .77                           1879-1963
    .78                           1963-1974.  Revolution
                              1974-    .  Independent
    .8                            General works
                                  Biography and memoirs
    .82                             Collective
    .83                             Individual, A-Z
    .9                      Local history and description, A-Z

                          e. g.  .B65  Bolama Island
```

West Africa.  West Coast
  Portuguese-speaking West Africa
   Local history and description - Continued
    Sao Tome and Principe

615     Periodicals.  Societies.  Serials
.18     General works
.2     Description and travel ⟶ *Social life + customs. Civilz.. Intell. lit.*
.3     Ethnography
.42      General works
.45      Individual elements in the population, A-Z

    History
.5     General works
     General special
      Foreign and general relations
       Class general works on the diplomatic
       history of a period with the period,
       e. g. DT615.65+.  For works on relations
       with a specific country regardless of
       period, see DT615.63
.62      General works
.63      Relations with individual countries, A-Z
       For list of countries, see pp. 212-214

    By period
.65     Early to 1522
.7     1522-1975.  Portuguese colony
.8     1975-    .  Independent

.9    Local history and description, A-Z

West Africa.　West Coast - Continued
　　　Spanish West Africa
　　　　　　Cf. DT330, Spanish Morocco
　　　　　　　　DT346.S7, Spanish Sahara
619　　　　　General works

　　　　　Equatorial Guinea (Spanish Guinea)
620　　　　　Periodicals.　Societies.　Serials
　.13　　　　Sources and documents
　.15　　　　Gazetteers.　Dictionaries, etc.
　.17　　　　Place names (General)
　　　　　　　For etymological studies, see PL8167.F3, etc.
　.2　　　　Guidebooks
　.22　　　　General works
　.23　　　　General special
　.24　　　　Views
　　　　　　Historic monuments, landmarks, scenery, etc.
　　　　　　　(General)
　　　　　　　　For local, see DT620.9
　.25　　　　　General works
　.26　　　　　Preservation
　.27　　　　Description and travel
　.3　　　　Antiquities
　　　　　　　For local antiquities, see DT620.9
　.4　　　　Social life and customs.　Civilization.　Intellectual
　　　　　　life
　　　　　　　For specific periods, see the period
　　　　　　Ethnography
　.42　　　　　General works
　.45　　　　　Individual elements in the population, A-Z

　　　　　　　.F35　Fang

　　　　　History
　.46　　　　Biography (Collective)
　　　　　　　　For individual biography, see the specific
　　　　　　　　　period or place
　.47　　　　Historiography
　.5　　　　General works

              **West Africa.  West Coast**
                **Spanish West Africa**
                  **Equatorial Guinea (Spanish Guinea)**
                    **History** - Continued
                      General special

| | |
|---|---|
| 620.6 | Political history |
| |     For specific periods, <u>see</u> the period |
| | Foreign and general relations |
| |     Class general works on the diplomatic |
| |       history of a period with the period, |
| |       e. g. DT620.65+.  For works on relations |
| |       with a specific country regardless of |
| |       period, <u>see</u> DT620.63 |
| .62 |     General works |
| .63 |     Relations with individual countries, A-Z |
| |       For list of countries, <u>see</u> pp. 212-214 |
| | **By period** |
| | Early to 1778 |
| |     Including Portuguese and Dutch claims |
| .65 |     General works |
| |     Biography and memoirs |
| .66 |       Collective |
| .67 |       Individual, A-Z |
| | 1778-1968 |
| .7 |     General works |
| |     Biography and memoirs |
| .72 |       Collective |
| .73 |       Individual, A-Z |
| | 1968- |
| .74 |     General works |
| |     1968-1979.  Regime of Macias Nguema |
| .75 |       General works |
| |       Biography and memoirs |
| .76 |         Collective |
| .77 |         Individual, A-Z |
| |     1979- |
| |       Including Revolution of 1979 |
| .8 |       General works |
| |       Biography and memoirs |
| .82 |         Collective |
| .83 |         Individual, A-Z |

West Africa.  West Coast
  Spanish West Africa
    Equatorial Guinea (Spanish Guinea) - Continued

620.9      Local history and description, A-Z
        For works on the mainland province of Rio Muni,
         see DT620+

      e. g.  .A65  Annobon Island (Pagalu)

        .E46  Elobey Islands
           Including Corisco, Cocotiers,
            Mbane and Conga

        .F47  Fernando Po (Macias Nguema Biyogo;
           Bioko)

Liberia
621     Periodicals.  Societies.  Serials
623     Gazetteers.  Dictionaries, etc.
  .3   Place names (General)
      For etymological studies, see PE3442.L5;
       PL8021.L5, etc.
  .5   Directories
  .7   Guidebooks
624     General works
       Description and travel
625       Through 1900
626       1901-1950
627       1951-
628     Antiquities
629     Social life and customs.  Civilization.  Intellectual
       life
       Ethnography
630       General works
  .5    Individual, A-Z

      e. g.  .K63  Kpelle

        .V2  Vei

        **West Africa.   West Coast**
          **Liberia** - Continued
             **History**

| | |
|---|---|
| 630.8 | Biography (Collective) |
| |    For individual biography, <u>see</u> the specific period or place |
| 631 | General works |
| | General special |
| |   Political history |
| .5 |    General works |
| |    By period, <u>see</u> the specific period |
| |   Foreign and general relations |
| 632 |    General works |
| |    By period, <u>see</u> the specific period |
| .5 |    Relations with individual countries, A-Z |
| |      For list of countries, <u>see</u> pp. 212-214 |

             **By period**

| | |
|---|---|
| | Early to 1847. Grain Coast. American Colonization Society settlements |
| 633 |   General works |
| |   Biography and memoirs |
| .2 |    Collective |
| .3 |    Individual, A-Z |
| |      e. g.   .A8  Ashmun, Jehudi |
| | 1847-1944. Republic of Liberia |
| 634 |   General works |
| |   Biography and memoirs |
| .2 |    Collective |
| .3 |    Individual, A-Z |
| |      e. g.   .R6  Roberts, Joseph Jenkins |
| | 1944-1971 |
| 635 |   General works |
| |   Biography and memoirs |
| .2 |    Collective |
| 636 |    Individual, A-Z |
| |      e. g.   .T8  Tubman, William V.S. |

                          West Africa.   West Coast
                            Liberia
                              History
                                By period - Continued
                                  1971-1980
636.2                               General works
                                    Biography and memoirs
  .3                                    Collective
  .4                                    Individual, A-Z

                                          e. g.   .T63  Tolbert, William R.


                                  1980-
  .5                                General works   *Incl. Civil War, 1989-*
                                    Biography and memoirs
  .52                                   Collective
  .53                                   Individual, A-Z


637                             Regions, towns, etc., A-Z

                                          e. g.   .G7  Grand Bassa County

                                                  .M6  Monrovia


639                         Congo (Kongo) River region
                              For works by Stanley, see DT351


                          Zaire.   Congo (Democratic Republic).   Belgian Congo
641                           Periodicals.  Societies.  Serials
643                           Dictionaries.  Guidebooks.  Directories
644                           General works
                              Description and travel
645                             Through 1880
646                             1881-1950
647                             1951-1980
  .5                            1981-
648                           Antiquities
649                           Social life and customs.  Civilization.  Intellectual
                                life

         West Africa.   West Coast
           Zaire.   Congo (Democratic Republic).   Belgian
               Congo - Continued
           Ethnography

| | | |
|---|---|---|
| 649.5 | | General works |
| 650 | | Individual elements in the population, A-Z |
| | .A48 | Alur |
| | .A93 | Azande |
| | .B33 | Bakongo |
| | .B34 | Balese |
| | | Baluba, _see_ .L8 |
| | .B36 | Bambute |
| | .B365 | Basakata |
| | .B366 | Bashi |
| | .B37 | Basku |
| | | Bassonge, _see_ .S55 |
| .U54 | .B375 | Bavili |
| | .B38 | Bayaka   _B44 Bemba_ |
| | .B57 | Bira |
| | .B66 | Boma |
| | .B87 | Bushongo |
| | .E45 | Ekonda |
| | .F43 | Flemings |
| | .G46 | Genya |
| | .H38 | Havu |
| | .H54 | Hima |
| | .H85 | _Hungana_ |
| | .K36 | Kasanga   _.K66 Kongo_ |
| | .K68 | Kota |
| | .K83 | Kuba |
| | .K86 | Kumu |
| | .L38 | Lele |
| | .L8 | Luba |
| | .L83 | Lulua |

West Africa.   West Coast
    Zaire.   Congo (Democratic Republic).   Belgian Congo
        Ethnography
650            Individual elements in the population,
              A-Z - Continued

| | |
|---|---|
| .M38 | Mayombe |
| .M42 | Mbala |
| .M46 | Mbole |
| .M64 | Monbuttus |
| .M65 | Mongo |
| .M97 | Muslims |
| .N34 | Nande |
| .N45 | Ngbaka |
| .N48 | Ngombe |
| .N85 | Ntomba |
| .P46 | Pende |
| .P94 | Pygmies |
| .S25 | Sanga |
| .S55 | Songe |
| .W33 | Wagenia |
| .W37 | Waregas |
| .Y3 | Yanzi |
| .Z44 | Zela |

West Africa. West Coast
  Zaire. Congo (Democratic Republic). Belgian
    Congo - Continued
   **History**
    Cf. DT31+, Partition of Africa
    Historiography

|  |  |
|---|---|
| 650.2 | General works |
|  | Biography of historians, area studies specialists, archaeologists, etc. |
| .3 | Collective |
| .4 | Individual, A-Z |
|  | Study and teaching |
| .7 | General works |
| .8 | By region or country, A-Z |
|  | Subarranged by author |
| 652 | General works |
|  | General special |
| 653 | Political history |
|  | For specific periods, <u>see</u> the period |
|  | Foreign and general relations |
|  | Class general works on the diplomatic history of a period with the period, e. g. DT654+. For relations with a specific country regardless of period, <u>see</u> DT653.5 |
| .3 | General works |
| .5 | Relations with individual countries, A-Z |
|  | For list of countries, <u>see</u> pp. 212-214 |

**By period**
  Early. Congo Kingdom. Portuguese claims.
    Association Internationale du Congo
     Cf. DT1357+, Angola

|  |  |
|---|---|
| 654 | General works |
|  | Biography and memoirs |
| .2 | Collective |
| .3 | Individual, A-Z |

    West Africa.   West Coast
      Zaire.   Congo (Democratic Republic).   Belgian Congo
        History
          **By period** - Continued
            Congo Free State, 1885-1908

|        |        |
|--------|--------|
| 655    | General works |
| .2     | Biography and memoirs |
|        | .A2A-Z  Collective |
|        | .A3-Z    Individual, A-Z |

            Belgian Congo, 1908-1960

|        |        |
|--------|--------|
| 657    | General works |
| .2     | Biography and memoirs |
|        | .A2A-Z  Collective |
|        | .A3-Z    Individual, A-Z |

            1960-

|        |        |
|--------|--------|
| 658    | General works |
| .2     | Biography and memoirs |
|        | .A2A-Z  Collective |
|        | .A3-Z    Individual, A-Z |
| .22    | Civil War, 1960-1965 |
|        |    Including assassination of Patrice Lumumba |
| .25    | 1965-    .  Regime of Mobuto Sese Seko |
|        |    Including Shaba Invasions of 1977 and 1978, and Kolwezi Massacre of 1978 |

| 663 | Biography and memoirs (Collective) |
|--------|--------|

West Africa.  West Coast
   Zaire.  Congo (Democratic Republic).  Belgian
     Congo - Continued
665         Local history and description, A-Z

               e. g.   .B3   Bas-Congo (Lower Congo)

                      .E4   Elisabethville.  Lubumbashi

                      .I55  Inkisi
                      .I8   Ituri Forest

                      .K28  Kasai
                      .K3   Katanga.  Shaba

                            Kinshasa, <u>see</u> .L4
                      .K55  Kisangani.  Stanleyville
                      .K58  Kivu

                      .L4   Leopoldville.  Kinshasa

                            Lubumbashi, <u>see</u> .E4

                      .M35  Maniema (Kasongo)

                            Shaba, <u>see</u> .K3
                            Stanleyville, <u>see</u> .K55

       **Islands**
669         General works
671         Individual islands or groups of islands, A-Z

              Annobon Islands, <u>see</u> DT620.9.A65

   .B58       Bissagos Islands (Ilhas dos Bijagós)
              Bolama, <u>see</u> DT613.9.B65

              Canary Islands, <u>see</u> DP302.C36+

West Africa.  West Coast
  Islands
671     Individual islands or groups of islands,
      A-Z - Continued

       Cape Verde
 .C2      Periodicals.  Societies.  Serials
 .C212     Guidebooks
 .C215     General works
 .C22      Description and travel
 .C23      Social life and customs.  Civilization.
        Intellectual life
       Ethnography
 .C242      General works
 .C245      Individual elements in the population, A-Z
       History
 .C25      General works
       By period
 .C265       Early to 1975
 .C28       1975-     .  Independent
 .C29     Local history and description, A-Z

      Elobey Islands, see DT620.9.E46
      Fernando Po, see DT620.9.F47

      Madeira, see DP702.M11+

 .S2     St. Helena

 .T8     Tristan da Cunha

(727-971)   Southern Africa, see DT1001+

## SOUTHERN AFRICA

| | |
|---|---|
| 1001 | Periodicals.  Societies.  Serials |
| | Museums, exhibitions, etc. |
| 1005 | General works |
| 1006 | Individual.  By place, A-Z |
| 1008 | Congresses |
| 1009 | Sources and documents |
| | Collected works (nonserial) |
| 1011 | Several authors |
| 1012 | Individual authors |
| 1014 | Gazetteers.  Dictionaries, etc. |
| 1015 | Place names (General) |
| 1016 | Directories |
| 1017 | Guidebooks |
| 1019 | General works |
| 1021 | General special |
| 1023 | Views |
| | Historic monuments, landmarks, scenery, etc. (General) |
| 1025 | General works |
| 1026 | Preservation |
| 1028 | Historical geography |
| | Description and travel |
| 1030 | Early through 1900 |
| 1032 | 1901-1950 |
| 1034 | 1951-1980 |
| 1036 | 1981- |
| 1050 | Antiquities |
| 1052 | Social life and customs.  Civilization.  Intellectual life |
| | For specific periods, see the period |
| | Ethnography |
| 1054 | General works |
| 1055 | National characteristics |
| 1056 | Ethnic and race relations |
| 1058 | Individual elements in the population, A-Z |

.B53  Blacks
.B75  British

.K56  Khoikhoi
.K86  !Kung
.M87  Muslims          .P63  Poles
.N58  Nguni
.S36  San

**Southern Africa** - Continued
**History**
        Periodicals.  Societies.  Serials, <u>see</u> DT1001

| | |
|---|---|
| 1062 | Dictionaries.  Chronological tables, outlines, etc. |
| 1064 | Biography (Collective) |
| | Historiography |
| 1066 |    General works |
| |    Biography of historians, area studies specialists, archaeologists, etc. |
| 1067 |       Collective |
| 1068 |       Individual, A-Z |
| | Study and teaching |
| 1070 |    General works |
| 1072 |    By region or country, A-Z |
| |       Subarranged by author |
| | General works |
| ~~1075~~ |    Through 1900 |
| ~~1077~~ |    1901-1975 |
| 1079 | *General works*    ~~1976~~ |
| 1090 | Pictorial works |
| 1092 | Juvenile works |
| | General special |
| 1093 |    Philosophy of Southern African history |
| 1095 |    History of several parts of Southern Africa treated together |
| 1096 |    Military history |
| | Political history |
| |    For specific periods, <u>see</u> the period |
| 1098 |    Sources and documents |
| 1099 |    General works |
| | Foreign and general relations |
| |    Class general works on the diplomatic history of a period with the period, e. g. DT1107+. For works on relations with a specific country regardless of period, <u>see</u> DT1105 |
| 1101 |    Sources and documents |
| 1103 |    General works |
| 1105 |    Relations with individual countries, A-Z |
| |       For list of countries, <u>see</u> pp. 212-214 |

               **Southern Africa**
                **History** - Continued
                 **By period**
                   Early to 1890

| | |
|---|---|
| 1107 | General works |
| | Biography and memoirs |
| |      Class biography under individual country |
| |      except for those persons who are associated |
| |      with more than one country, or who inhabited |
| |      a region that does not correspond to a |
| |      modern jurisdiction |
| 1109 |      Collective |
| 1110 |      Individual, A-Z |
| | Individual empires |
| 1111 |      Karanga Empire |
| 1113 |      Monomotapa |
| 1115 |      Nguni States |
| 1117 |      Rozwi Kingdoms |
| 1119 |      Zulu Empire |
| |         Cf. DT2400.Z85, Zululand |
| 1123 | Mfecane, ca. 1820-ca. 1840 |
| |      For Mfecane in individual countries, <u>see</u> |
| |      the country |
| | 1890-1975 |
| 1125 | Periodicals. Societies. Serials |
| 1126 | Sources and documents |
| 1128 | Historiography |
| 1130 | General works |
| 1132 | Social life and customs. Civilization. |
| |      Intellectual life |
| 1135 | Military history |
| 1137 | Political history |
| 1139 | Foreign and general relatins |
| 1142 | Biography and memoirs (Collective) |
| 1144 | 1890-1918 |
| 1145 | 1918-1945 |
| 1147 | 1945-1976 |
| | 1975- |
| 1155 | Periodicals. Societies. Serials |
| 1157 | Congresses |
| 1159 | Sources and documents |
| 1161 | Collected works (nonserial) |
| 1163 | Historiography |

Southern Africa
  History
    By period
      1975-    - Continued

| | |
|---|---|
| 1165 | General works |
| 1166 | General special |
| 1168 | Social life and customs. Civilization. Intellectual life |
| 1170 | Military history |
| 1172 | Foreign and general relations |
| 1174 | Biography and memoirs (Collective) |
| 1177 | National liberation movements |
| 1190 | Local history and description, A-Z |

      e. g.   .K35  Kalahari Desert

             .L56  Limpopo River and Valley

             .Z36  Zambezi River and Valley

## ANGOLA

| | |
|---|---|
| 1251 | Periodicals. Societies. Serials |
| 1259 | Sources and documents |
| 1264 | Gazetteers. Dictionaries, etc. |
| 1265 | Place names (General) |
| 1267 | Guidebooks |
| 1269 | General works |
| 1271 | General special |
| 1275 | Historic monuments, landmarks, scenery, etc. (General) |
| |    For local, see DT1450+ |
| | Description and travel |
| 1282 |   Early through 1980 |
| 1286 |   1981- |
| 1300 | Antiquities |
| |    For local antiquities, see DT1450+ |
| 1302 | Social life and customs. Civilization. Intellectual life |
| |    For specific periods, see the period |

Angola - Continued
   Ethnography
1304      General works
1306      Ethnic and race relations
1308      Individual elements in the population, A-Z

        .C67   Chokwe

        .H35   Hanya
        .H48   Herero
        .H56   Himba

        .K66   Kongo
        .K83   Kuanyama

        .L84   Luena
        .L86   Lunda

        .M38   Mbundu
        .M85   Mwila

        .N46   Ndonga
        .N53   Ngangela
        .N58   Nkumbi
        .N93   Nyaneka

        .O83   Ovambo
        .P68   Portuguese
        .S35   San
        .S68   Sosso

**History**
   Periodicals. Societies. Serials, <u>see</u> DT1251
1314    Biography (Collective)
      For individual biography, <u>see</u> the specific
        period
   Historiography
1316     General works
    Biography of historians, area studies specialists,
        archaeologists, etc.
1317      Collective
1318      Individual, A-Z
1325    General works

```
                        Angola
                          History - Continued
                            General special
1348                          Political history
                                For specific periods, see the period
                              Foreign and general relations
                                Class general works on the diplomatic history
                                    of a period with the period, e. g. DT1357+.
                                    For works on relations with a specific
                                    country regardless of period, see DT1355
1353                          General works
1355                          Relations with individual countries, A-Z
                                For list of countries, see pp. 212-214 __

                          By period
                            Early to 1648
                                Cf. DT654+, Congo (Kingdom)
1357                          General works
                              Biography and memoirs
1359                            Collective
1365                            Individual, A-Z


                                    e. g.   .D53  Dias de Novais, Paulo


                                            .N56  Ngola Inene, King of Ndongo
                                            .N95  Nzinga, Queen of Matamba


1367                          Period of conquest, 1575-1683
1369                          Dutch occupation, 1641-1648
                            1648-1885.   Portuguese expansion
                                Cf. DT654+, Congo (Kingdom)
1373                          General works
                              Biography and memoirs
1375                            Collective
1376                            Individual, A-Z


                                    e. g.   .S56  Silva Porto, Francisco da


1378                          Mbwila, Battle of, 1665
1380                          Pungua-Ndongo, Siege of, 1671
1382                          Separatist revolt, 1823
```

**Angola**
  **History**
    **By period** - Continued
      1885-1961.  Portuguese consolidation

|  |  |
|---|---|
| 1385 | General works |
|  | Biography and memoirs |
| 1387 | Collective |
| 1388 | Individual, A-Z |

          e. g.   .K35  Kalandula, Bailundo King

                 .M88  Mutu ya Kevela

|  |  |
|---|---|
| 1390 | Dembo rebellions, 1877-1919 |
| 1392 | Bailundo War, 1902 |
| 1394 | Mussorongo revolt, 1908 |
| 1396 | Bakongo rebellion, 1913-1914 |
|  | 1961-1975.  Revolution |
| 1398 | Periodicals.  Societies.  Serials |
| 1400 | Sources and documents |
| 1402 | General works |
|  | Military history |
| 1405 | General works |
| 1406 | Individual events, battles, etc., A-Z |

          e. g.   .L83  Luanda Uprising, 1961

          Foreign participation

|  |  |
|---|---|
| 1408 | General works |
| 1410 | By region or country, A-Z |

          e. g.   .C83  Cuba

|  |  |
|---|---|
| 1413 | Special topics, A-Z |
|  | Biography and memoirs |
| 1415 | Collective |
| 1417 | Individual, A-Z |

          e. g.   .A54  Andrade, Mario Pinto de

                 .C55  Chipenda, Daniel

                 .R63  Roberto, Holden

              **Angola**
                **History**
                    **By period** - Continued
                        1975-      .   Independent
                            For South African raids on SWAPO installations,
                                1978-      , <u>see</u> DT1645

| | |
|---|---|
| 1420 | General works |
| | Biography and memoirs |
| 1422 | Collective |
| 1424 | Individual, A-Z |

                         e. g.   .A58   Alves, Nito

                                .S38   Savimbi, Jonas

| | |
|---|---|
| 1426 | Agostinho Neto.   1975-1979 |
| |     Class here general works on life and administration |
| 1428 | Civil War, 1975- |
| 1430 | South African invasion, 1975-1976 |
| 1432 | Coup d'etat, 1977 |
| 1434 | Jose Eduardo dos Santos, 1979- |
| |     Class here general works on life and administration |
| 1436 | South African incursions, 1978- 1990 |
| |     Including Lusaka Accord |

              **Local history and description**

| | |
|---|---|
| 1450 | Provinces, districts, regions, etc., A-Z |

                       e. g.   .B54   Bié

                                .C33   Cabinda
                                .C85   Cunene River

                                .H83   Huambo
                                .H85   Huila

                                .K83   Kwanza (Cuanza) River

                                .M69   Moxico
                                .N36   Namibe Province.   Moçâmides

                                .U55   Uige
                                .Z35   Zaire Province

**Angola**
    **Local history and description** - Continued
        Cities, towns, etc.

| | |
|---|---|
| 1455 | Luanda |
| 1465 | Other cities, towns, etc., A-Z |

      e. g.   .B35   Bailundo.   Teixeira da Silva
                .B46   Benguela

                .C55   Chibia.   João de Almeida

                .H83   Huambo.   Nova Lisboa

                .K38   Kassinga.   Cassinga
                .K85   Kuito.   Bié.   Silva Porto

                .L73   Lobito
                .L83   Luachimo.   Portugália

                .L84   Luao.   Teixeira de Sousa
                .L85   Lubango.   Sá da Bandeira
                .L86   Luena.   Luso

                .M35   Malange.   Malanje
                .M42   Mbanza.   Kongo.   Sao Salvador do
                      Congo
                .M46   Menongue.   Serpa Pinto

                .N36   Namibe.   Moçâmides
                .N55   Ngiva.   Pereira de Eça

                .N58   Ngunza.   Novo Redondo
                .N94   Nzeto.   Ambrizete

                .S38   Saurimo.   Henrique de Carvalho

                .U55   Uíge.   Carmona

## NAMIBIA.   SOUTH-WEST AFRICA

| | |
|---|---|
| 1501 | Periodicals. Societies. Serials |
| 1509 | Sources and documents |
| 1514 | Gazetteers. Dictionaries, etc. |
| 1515 | Place names (General) |
| 1517 | Guidebooks |
| 1519 | General works |
| 1521 | General special |
| 1523 | Views |
| | Historic monuments, landmarks, scenery, etc. (General) |
| |     For local, <u>see</u> DT1650+ |
| | Description and travel |
| 1532 |   Through 1980 |
| 1536 |   1981- |
| 1550 | Antiquities |
| |     For local antiquities, <u>see</u> DT1650+ |
| 1552 | Social life and customs. Civilization. Intellectual life |
| |     For specific periods, <u>see</u> the period |
| | Ethnography |
| 1554 |   General works |
| 1555 |   Ethnic and race relations |
| 1556 |   Apartheid |
| 1557 |   Blacks |
| |      Including Homelands |
| 1558 |   Individual elements in the population, A-Z |
| | |
| |    .A46   Afrikaners |
| |    .B65   Bondelswarts |
| | |
| |    .G46   Germans |
| | |
| |    .H45   Heikum |
| |    .H47   Herero |
| |    .H56   Himba |
| | |
| |    .K83   Kuanyama |

Namibia.   South-West Africa
    Ethnography
1558        Individual elements in the population, A-Z - Continued

          .M33  Mbandieru

          .M37  Mbukushu

          .N36  Nama

          .N46  Ndonga

          .O83  Ovambo

          .R45  Rehoboth Basters

          .S36  Sambyu

          .S38  San

**History**
    Periodicals.  Societies.  Serials, see DT1501
1564    Biography (Collective)
        For individual biography, see the specific
          period
    Historiography
1566      General works
      Biography of historians, area studies specialists,
        archaeologists, etc.
1567        Collective
1568        Individual, A-Z
1575  General works

  General special
1579    Political history
      For specific periods, see the period
    Foreign and general relations
      Class general works on the diplomatic history
        of a period with the period, e. g. DT1587+.
        For works on relations with a specific
        country regardless of period, see DT1585
1583    General works
1585    Relations with individual countries, A-Z
      For list of countries, see pp. 212-214

                    Namibia.   South-West Africa
                      History - Continued
                        By period
                          Early to 1884
                              Including Portuguese, Dutch, and British
                                 claims, and German and British settlements
1587                          General works
                              Biography and memoirs
1589                            Collective
1595                            Individual, A-Z

                                      e. g.   .J36   Jan Jonker Afrikaner

                                              .J66   Jonker Afrikaner

1597                          Rehoboth Basters' settlement, 1868
1599                          Walvis Bay annexation, 1878
1601                          Afrikaaner Trek, 1878-1879
                          1884-1915.   German South-West Africa
                              Including Luderitz concessions
1603                          General works
                              Biography and memoirs
1605                            Collective
1608                            Individual, A-Z

                                      e. g.   .C57   Christian, Johannes

                                              .M35   Maharero, Samuel
                                              .M67   Morenga

                                              .W58   Witbooi, Hendrik

1610                          Afrikaaner Republic of Upingtonia, 1885-1887
1612                          Witbooi Rebellion, 1893-1894
1614                          Herero Uprising, 1896
1616                          Bondelswarts' Uprising, 1903-1904
1618                          Herero War, 1904-1907
1620                          Nama War, 1904-1906
1622                          Rehoboth Basters Uprising, 1915

Namibia.   South-West Africa
  History
    By period - Continued
      1915-1946.   South African Mandate under authority
        of the League of Nations

| | |
|---|---|
| 1625 | General works |
| | Biography and memoirs |
| 1627 |   Collective |
| 1628 |   Individual, A-Z |

          .C57   Christian, Jacobus

          .M78   Morris, Abraham

| | |
|---|---|
| 1630 | Bondelswarts' Rebellion, 1922 |
| 1632 | Rehoboth Basters' Rebellion, 1925 |
| 1634 | Angola Afrikaaners' resettlement, 1925 |
| 1636 | German reunification movement, 1932-1939 |

      1946-    .   United Nations Trusteeship.   South
        African administration

| | |
|---|---|
| 1638 | General works |
| | Biography and memoirs |
| 1640 |   Collective |
| 1641 |   Individual, A-Z |

         e. g.  .K36   Kapuuo, Clemens
               .K88   Kutako, Hosea

               .M84   Mudge, Dirk
               .N85   Nujoma, Sam

               .T75   Toivo ja Toivo, Andimba

               .W58   Witbooi, David

| | |
|---|---|
| 1643 | Cancellation of South African Mandate, 1966 |
| 1645 | Armed struggle for national liberation, 1966- |
| |   Including South African raids on SWAPO |
| |     installations in Angola, 1978- |
| 1647 | Turnhalle conference, 1975- |
| 1648 | Transitional government, 1985- |

Namibia.   South-West Africa - Continued
**Local history and description**
1670       Provinces, regions, etc., A-Z

             e. g.    .C36  Caprivi Strip
                      .D36  Damaraland

                      .E86  Etosha Pan
                      .H47  Hereroland

                      .K37  Kaokoland
                      .K38  Kavango

                      .N36  Namaland
                      .N37  Namib Desert

                      .O63  Okavango River and Swamp
                      .O83  Owambo

                      .S64  Skeleton Coast
                      .S83  Swakop River and Valley

          Cities, towns, etc.
1680         Windhoek
1685         Other cities, towns, etc., A-Z

             e. g.    .B48  Bethanie

                      .K37  Karasburg

                      .L84  Luderitz.   Luderitzbucht

                      .R46  Rehoboth

                      .S83  Swakopmund

                      .W35  Walvis Bay (South Africa)

## SOUTH AFRICA

| | |
|---|---|
| 1701 | Periodicals. Societies. Serials |
| | Museums, exhibitions, etc. |
| 1705 | General works |
| 1706 | Individual. By place, A-Z |
| 1708 | Congresses |
| 1709 | Sources and documents |
| 1712 | Collected works (nonserial) |
| 1714 | Gazetteers. Dictionaries, etc. |
| 1715 | Place names (General) |
| 1716 | Directories |
| 1717 | Guidebooks |
| 1719 | General works |
| 1721 | General special |
| 1723 | Views |
| | Historic monuments, landmarks, scenery, etc. (General) |
| |     For local, see DT2400, DT2405, etc. |
| 1725 | General works |
| 1726 | Preservation |
| | Description and travel |
| 1730 | Early through 1800 |
| 1732 | 1801-1900 |
| 1734 | 1901-1950 |
| 1736 | 1951-1965 |
| 1738 | 1966- |
| 1750 | Antiquities |
| |     For local antiquities, see DT2400, DT2405, etc. |
| 1752 | Social life and customs. Civilization. Intellectual life |
| |     For specific periods, see the period |
| | **Ethnography** |
| 1754 | General works |
| 1755 | National characteristics |
| 1756 | Race relations |
| 1757 | Apartheid |
| | Blacks |
| |     For works dealing collectively with the Bantu-speaking folk societies of South Africa, see GN656+ |
| 1758 | General works |
| 1760 | Homelands |
| |     For individual Homelands, see DT2400.B66, etc. |

**South Africa**
  **Ethnography** - Continued
1762     Afro-Afrikaner relations
1768     Individual elements in the population, A-Z

    .A57  Afrikaners
    .A85  Asians

    .B35  Bafokeng
    .B53  Bhaca
         Blacks, <u>see</u> DT1758
         Boers, <u>see</u> .A57
         Bushmen, <u>see</u> .S36

    .C55  Chinese
    .C65  Colored people
    .C68  Cornish
    .C87  Croats
    .C94  Czechs

    .D88  Dutch
    .E38  East Indians

    .F54  Fingos
    .F56  Flemish
    .F73  French
           Including Huguenots

    .G48  Germans
    .G56  Ghoya
    .G74  Griquas
         Hottentots, <u>see</u> .K56

    .J37  Japanese
    .K53  Kgatla
    .K56  Khoikhoi
    .K68  Korana

    .M35  Malays
    .M36  Mamabolo
    .M38  Mashona

South Africa
Ethnography
1768          Individual elements in the population, A-Z - Continued

.N37   Nama
.N38   Naron

.P44   Pedi
.P53   Phalaborwa
.P66   Pondos
.P67   Portuguese

.R45   Rehoboth Basters
.R65   Rolong

.S36   San
.S43   Scandinavians
.S68   Sotho

.T36   Tamils
.T46   Tembu

.T55   Thonga
.T57   Tlhaping
.T89   Tswana

.V45   Venda
.W55   Whites

.X57   Xhosa

.Z95   Zulu

1770          South Africans in foreign countries (General)
                   For South Africans in a particular country,
                   see the country

South Africa - Continued
  History
       Periodicals.  Societies.  Serials, see DT1701

| | |
|---|---|
| 1772 | Dictionaries.  Chronological tables, outlines, etc. |
| 1774 | Biography (Collective) |
| | Historiography |
| 1776 |   General works |
| |   Biography of historians, area studies specialists, archaeologists, etc. |
| 1777 |     Collective |
| 1778 |     Individual, A-Z |
| | Study and teaching |
| 1780 |   General works |
| 1782 |   By region or country, A-Z |
| 1787 | General works |
| ~~1784~~ | ~~Through 1983~~ |
| ~~1787~~ | ~~1984-~~ |
| | General special |
| 1796 |   Military history |
| |     For specific periods, see the period |
| 1798 |   Political history |
| |     For specific periods, see the period |
| |   Foreign and general relations |
| |     Class general works on the diplomatic history of a period with the period, e. g. DT1807+.  For works on relations with a specific country regardless of period, see DT1805 |
| 1803 |     General works |
| 1805 |     Relations with individual countries, A-Z |
| |       For list of countries, see pp. 212-214 |

  **By period**
    Early to 1652

| | |
|---|---|
| 1807 |   General works |
| |   Biography and memoirs |
| 1809 |     Collective |
| 1810 |     Individual, A-Z |

           **South Africa**
             **History**
               **By period** - Continued
                  1652-1795.  Dutch East India Company administration

|  |  |
|---|---|
| 1813 | General works |
|  | Biography and memoirs |
| 1816 | Collective |
| 1817 | Individual, A-Z |

                      e. g.   .P53   Phalo, Xhosa chief

                                .S84   Stel, Simon van der

                                .V35   Van Riebeeck, Jan

|  |  |
|---|---|
| 1819 | First Khoikhoi War, 1659 |
| 1821 | Second Khoikhoi War, 1673-1677 |
| 1823 | Huguenot settlement, 1688 |
| 1825 | Xhosa Wars, 1779-1802 |

                  1795-1836.  British possession

|  |  |
|---|---|
| 1828 | General works |
|  | Biography and memoirs |
| 1830 | Collective |
| 1831 | Individual, A-Z |

                      e. g.   .C53   Chaka, Zulu chief

                                .D56   Dingiswayo, Zulu chief

                                .G35   Gaika, Xhosa chief

|  |  |
|---|---|
| 1835 | Graaf-Reinet and Swellendam Rebellion, 1795 |
| 1837 | Frontier Wars, 1811-1878 |
| 1839 | Slaghter's Nek incident, 1815 |
| 1840 | British settlers, 1820 |
| 1841 | Mfecane.  Difaqanee, ca. 1821-1840 |
| 1843 | Fiftieth Ordinance, 1828 |
| 1845 | Abolition of slavery, 1834 |

**South Africa**
  **History**
    **By period** - Continued
      1836-1910.  British consolidation

| | |
|---|---|
| 1848 | General works |
| | Biography and memoirs |
| 1850 | Collective |
| 1851 | Individual, A-Z |

        e. g.   .C48   Ceteshwayo, Zulu chief

                .D56   Dingaan, Zulu chief
                .D57   Dinuzulu, Zulu chief

                .J36   Jameson, Leander Starr
                .K89   Kruger, Paul

                .M55   Milner, Alfred
                .P35   Panda, Zulu chief

                .R56   Rhodes, Cecil John
                .S37   Sarhili, Xhosa chief

| | |
|---|---|
| 1853 | Great Trek, 1836-1840 |
| |   For individual treks, <u>see</u> DT2120, DT2242, etc. |
| |   For Battle of Blood River, <u>see</u> DT2247.B56 |
| 1855 | War of the Axe, 1846-1848.  Seventh Xhosa War |
| 1857 | Annexation of British Kaffraria, 1847 |
| 1859 | Kat River Rebellion, 1851 |
| 1861 | German colonization, 1856 |
| 1863 | Xhosa cattle killing.  Vision of Nongquase, 1856-1857 |
| 1865 | First Basuto War, 1858 |
| 1867 | East Indians arrive, 1860 |
| 1869 | Second Basuto War, 1865-1866 |
| 1871 | Diamond rush begins, 1867 |
| 1873 | Third Basuto War, 1867-1868 |

         South Africa
           History
             By period
               1836-1910. British consolidation - Continued
                 Zulu War, 1879

| | |
|---|---|
| 1875 | General works |
| 1877 | Personal narratives |
| 1879 | Individual events, battles, etc., A-Z |

                   e. g.    .I83   Isandhlwana, Battle of

                          .K36   Kambula, Battle of

                          .R68   Rorke's Drift, Battle of

                          .U58   Ulundi, Battle of

| | |
|---|---|
| 1882 | Special topics, A-Z |
| 1884 | Transkei Revolt, 1880 |
| 1886 | Annexation of Griqualand, 1880 |
| 1888 | Rand Gold rush begins, 1886 |
| 1889 | Jameson Raid, 1895 |

                 South African War, 1899-1902

| | |
|---|---|
| 1890 | Periodicals. Societies. Serials |
| 1892 | Sources and documents |
| 1894 | Causes |
| 1896 | General works |
| 1898 | Pictorial works |

                 <u>Military history</u>, *General works*

| | |
|---|---|
| *1899* | British Army |
| 1900 | General works |
| 1902 | Regimental histories |
| |     Subarranged by author |
| | Afrikaner Army |
| 1904 | General works |
| 1906 | Regimental histories |
| |     Subarranged by author |

                  **South Africa**
                    **History**
                        **By period**
                            1836-1910.  British possession
                              South African War, 1899-1902
                                Military history - Continued

1908                                   Individual events, battles, etc., A-Z

                          e. g.   .C65  Colenso, Battle of, 1899

                                  .K56  Kimberley, Siege of, 1899-1900
                                  .L34  Ladysmith, Siege of, 1899-1900

                                  .M34  Mafeking, Siege of, 1899-1900
                                  .M35  Magersfontein, Battle of,
                                              1899

                                .S87  Stormberg, Battle of, 1899

                              Foreign participation
1911                                 General works
1913                                 By region or country, A-Z
                            Personal narratives
1915                                   Collective
1916                                 Individual, A-Z
1918                           Special topics, A-Z

                              .M44  Medical care

                              .P75  Prisoners and prisons
                              .P83  Public opinion
                              *.R44  Religious aspects*
1920                               Peace of Vereeniging, 1902

                          1902-1910
1921                               General works
1922                               Importation of Chinese laborers, 1904

South Africa
  History
    By period - Continued
      1910-1961.  Union of South Africa

| | |
|---|---|
| 1924 | General works |
| | Biography and memoirs |
| 1926 | Collective |
| 1927 | Individual, A-Z |

        e. g.  .A34  Abdurahman, A.

              .D83  Dube, J.L.

              .H47  Herzog, J.B.M.
              .J33  Jabavu, J.T.

              .M35  Malan, Daniel
              .M85  Msimang, Selby

              .P53  Plaatje, Sol

              .S46  Seme, P. Ka I.
              .S68  Smuts, Jan Christiaan

      1910-1948

| | |
|---|---|
| 1928 | General works |
| 1929 | Civil disobedience campaigns by Mohandas Gandhi, 1906-1914 |
| 1931 | Founding of South African Native National Congress, 1912 |
| 1933 | Afrikaner Rebellion, 1914 |
| 1935 | Rand Revolt, 1922 |
| 1937 | Founding of National Party, 1934 |
| .5 | Afrikaner centennial, 1936-1938 |

      1948-1961.  Afrikaner domination

| | |
|---|---|
| 1938 | General works |
| 1939 | Pass law demonstrations, 1956 |
| 1941 | Sharpeville Massacre, 1960 |

      **South Africa**
        **History**
          **By period** - Continued
            1961-   .   Republic of South Africa

                For raids on SWAPO installations in Angola,
                    <u>see</u> DT1645
                For South African invasion of Angola, <u>see</u>
                    DT1436
                For Nkomati Accord, <u>see</u> DT3396

| | |
|---|---|
| 1945 | General works |
| | Biography and memoirs |
| 1948 |    Collective |
| 1949 |    Individual, A-Z |

                   e. g.  .B55  Biko, Steve
                         .B88  Buthelezi, Gatsha

                         .L88  Luthuli, Albert

                     (.M35  Mandela, Nelson  see DT 1974)
                      .M36  Mandela, Winnie
                      .M38  Matanzima, Kaiser
                      .M85  Mulder, Cornelius (Connie)

                      .S58  Sisulu, Walter
                      .T36  Tambo, Oliver

| | |
|---|---|
| 1951 | Hendrik Verwoerd, 1961-1966 |
| |    Class here general works on life and administration |
| 1953 | National liberation and armed struggle by ANC begins, 1961- |
| 1955 | Rivonia Trial, 1964 |
| 1957 | Balthazar Johannes Vorster, 1966-1978 |
| |    Class here general works on life and administration |
| 1959 | Soweto uprising, 1976 |
| 1961 | Mulder scandal, 1978 |
| 1963 | Pieter Willem Botha, 1978- |
| |    Class here general works on life and administration |
| 1965 | Sharpeville Massacre Anniversary, 1985 |
| 1967 | State of emergency, 1985- |
| 1969 | Soweto uprising anniversary, 1986 |
| *1970* | *F. W. de Klerk, 1989-1994* |
| | *Class here general works on life and administration (List 242)* |
| *1974* | *Nelson Mandela, 1994-* |
| | *Class her ...* |

          **South Africa - Continued**
           **Local history and description**
             **Cape Province.  Cape of Good Hope**

| | |
|---|---|
| 1991 | Periodicals.  Societies.  Serials |
| 1999 | Sources and documents |
| 2002 | Collected works (nonserial) |
| 2004 | Gazetteers.  Dictionaries, etc. |
| 2005 | Place names (General) |
| 2006 | Directories |
| 2007 | Guidebooks |
| 2009 | General works |
| 2020 | Description and travel |
| 2027 | Social life and customs.  Civilization.  Intellectual life |
| |     For specific periods, <u>see</u> the period |
| 2032 | Ethnography.  Race relations |
| | **History** |
| |   Periodicals.  Societies.  Serials, <u>see</u> DT1991 |
| 2035 |   Biography (Collective) |
| |     For individual biography, <u>see</u> the specific period |
| 2037 |   Historiography |
| 2039 |   General works |
| |   **By period** |
| |     Early to 1795, <u>see</u> DT1807+ |
| |     1795-1872 |
| 2042 |       General works |
| |       Biography and memoirs |
| 2043 |         Collective |
| 2044 |         Individual, A-Z |
| |     1872-1910 |
| 2046 |       General works |
| |       Biography and memoirs |
| 2048 |         Collective |
| 2049 |         Individual, A-Z |
| |     1910- |
| 2051 |       General works |
| |       Biography and memoirs |
| 2053 |         Collective |
| 2054 |         Individual, A-Z |

South Africa
Local history and description - Continued
Orange Free State.  Oranje Vrystaat
2075            Periodicals.  Societies.   Serials
2079            Sources and documents
2082            Collected works (nonserial)
2084            Gazetteers.  Dictionaries, etc.
2085            Place names (General)
2086            Directories
2087            Guidebooks
2089            General works
2090            Description and travel
2097            Social life and customs.  Civilization.
                    Intellectual life
                        For specific periods, see the period
2102            Ethnography.  Race relations

                History
                        For conflicts with the Sotho, the Napier
                            Treaty and Warden Line, see DT2630+
                        For Great Trek, see DT1853
                        Periodicals.  Societies.  Serials, see DT2075
2105            Biography (Collective)
2109            General works

                By period
                    Early to 1854.  Transorangia
                        For Batlokwa Uprising, 1822, see DT2630
2112                General works
                    Biography and memoirs
2113                    Collective
2114                    Individual, A-Z
2116                Griqua settlements, 1803
2118                1818-1829.  Mfecane.  Difaqane
2120                1837-1848.  Treks into Transorangia
2122                1848-1854.  Orange River sovereignty

```
                    South Africa
                      Local history and description
                        Orange Free State.  Oranje Vrystaat
                          History
                            By period - Continued
                              1854-1910
                                  Cf. DT2630, General boundary disputes
                                      with Basutoland
                                  For South African War, 1899-1902, see
                                      DT1890+
                                  For diamond discoveries, see DT1871
2124                              General works
                                  Biography and memoirs
2126                                Collective
2127                                Individual, A-Z

                                      e. g.  .B83  Brand, Johannes Henricus

                                             .K65  Kok, Adam III

                                             .S84  Steyn, M.T.

2129                              War against the Sotho, 1858
                                      Cf. DT2630, Lesotho
2131                              Purchase of Griqua lands, 1861
2133                              War against the Sotho, 1865-1866
                                      Cf. DT2636, Lesotho's wars with the
                                          Orange Free State
2135                              Treaty of Aliwal North and cession of
                                      Sotho lands, 1869
2137                              Black Flag revolt, 1875
2139                              Orange River Colony, 1900-1910

                              1910-
2142                              General works
                                  Biography and memoirs
2144                                Collective
2145                                Individual, A-Z
```

           **South Africa**
            **Local history and description** - Continued
              **Natal**

| | |
|---|---|
| 2181 | Periodicals. Societies. Serials |
| 2189 | Sources and documents |
| 2192 | Collected works (nonserial) |
| 2194 | Gazetteers. Dictionaries, etc. |
| 2195 | Place names (General) |
| 2196 | Directories |
| 2197 | Guidebooks |
| 2199 | General works |
| 2205 | Views |
| 2210 | Description and travel |
| 2217 | Social life and customs. Civilization. Intellectual life |
| | For specific periods, <u>see</u> the period |
| 2222 | Ethnography. Race relations |

              **History**
                Periodicals. Societies. Serials, <u>see</u> DT2181

| | |
|---|---|
| 2225 | Biography (Collective) |
| | For individual biography, <u>see</u> the specific period |
| 2227 | Historiography |
| 2229 | General works |

              **By period**
                Early to 1843

| | |
|---|---|
| 2232 | General works |
| | Biography and memoirs |
| 2234 | Collective |
| 2235 | Individual, A-Z |

                    e. g.   .R48  Retief, Piet

| | |
|---|---|
| 2238 | Mfecane (Difaqane) beginnings, 1818-1843 |
| 2240 | British settlement, 1824 |
| 2242 | Treks into Natal, 1837-1846 |
| | Cf. DT1853, Great Trek |

       South Africa
         Local history and description
           Natal
             History
               By period
                 Early to 1843 - Continued
                   War with Dingaan, 1837-1840
                     Including death of Piet Retief

2245                      General works
2247                      Special events, battles, etc., A-Z

                                 e. g.   .B56   Blood River, Battle of,
                                             1838

                                      .M36   Magongo, Battle of, 1840

                 1843-1910.  British colony
                   For works on the Zulu war, 1879, <u>see</u>
                     DT1875+
                   For works on the South African War,
                     1899-1902, <u>see</u> DT1890+
2250                      General works
                   Biography and memoirs
2252                       Collective
2254                       Individual, A-Z

                                 e. g.   .K43   Keate, R.W.

                                      .S54   Shepstone, Theophilus

2257                      Langalibalele Rebellion, 1873
2259                      Pedi War, 1879
2261                      Incorporation of Zululand and Tongaland,
                     1897
2263                      Anti-Asian riots, 1897
2265                      Annexation of Vryheid, Utrecht, and
                     Wakkerstroom, 1902
2267                      Bambata Rebellion, 1907
                 1910-
2270                      General works
                   Biography and memoirs
2272                       Collective
2273                       Individual, A-Z
2275                      Zulu-Indian riots, 1949
2278                      Kwazulu-Natal Indaba, 1986-

South Africa
Local history and description - Continued
Transvaal. South African Republic

| | |
|---|---|
| 2291 | Periodicals. Societies. Serials |
| 2299 | Sources and documents |
| 2302 | Collected works (nonserial) |
| 2304 | Gazetteers. Dictionaries, etc. |
| 2305 | Place names (General) |
| 2306 | Directories |
| 2307 | Guidebooks |
| 2309 | General works |
| 2310 | Description and travel |
| 2317 | Social life and customs. Civilization. Intellectual life |
| | For specific periods, see the period |
| 2322 | Ethnography. Race relations |
| | **History** |
| | Periodicals. Societies. Serials, see DT2292 |
| 2325 | Biography (Collective) |
| | For individual biography, see the specific period |
| 2329 | General works |
| | **By period** |
| | Early to 1857 |
| 2332 | General works |
| | Biography and memoirs |
| 2334 | Collective |
| 2335 | Individual, A-Z |

e. g.  .M36  Mantatisi (Mantatee)

.P68  Potgieter, A.H.

.P84  Pretorius, Andries

| | |
|---|---|
| 2338 | Batlokwa uprising under Mantatisi, 1922 |
| 2340 | Ndebele in Transvaal under Mzilikazi, 1822-1837 |
| | Cf. DT2951, Mzilikazi's invasion and occupation of Zimbabwe |
| 2342 | Treks into Transvaal, 1837-1852 |
| 2344 | Sand River Convention, 1852 |

```
                    South Africa
                      Local history and description
                        Transvaal.   South African Republic
                          History
                            By period - Continued
                              1857-1880.   South African Republic
        2347                      General works
                                  Biography and memoirs
        2349                        Collective
        2350                        Individual, A-Z

                                        e. g.   .B88  Burgers, T.F.

                                                .J68  Joubert, W.F.

                                                .N53  Njabel
                                                .P84  Pretorius, M.W.

                                                .S45  Sekhukhune

        2352                      Pedi uprising under Sekhukhune, 1876-1877
                                  War of 1880-1881.   First Anglo-Afrikaner War
        2354                        General works
        2357                        Personal narratives
        2359                        Individual events, battles, etc., A-Z

                                        e. g.   .I65  Ingogo, Battle of, 1881

                                                .L35  Laing's Nek, Battle of,
                                                        1880
                                                .M36  Majuba Hill, Battle of,
                                                        1881

                              1881-1910
                                  For Witwaterwrand gold discovery, see DT1888
                                  For Jameson raid, see DT1889
        2361                      General works
                                  Biography and memoirs
        2363                        Collective
        2364                        Individual, A-Z
        2366                      Stellaland and Goshen, 1882-1884
                                      Cf. DT2483, Botswana
        2368                      Venda War, 1898
```

South Africa
Local history and description
Transvaal.   South African Republic
History
By period - Continued
2371                      1902-1910.  British Crown Colony
1910-
2375                          General works
Biography and memoirs
2377                              Collective
2378                              Individual, A-Z
2400             Other regions, districts, etc., A-Z

e. g.    .B66   Boputhatswana

.C58   Ciskei
.D83   Drakensburg Mountains

.G39   Gazankulu
.G84   Great Karoo
Homelands (General), see DT1760
.K35   Kaffraria
.K36   KaNgwana
.K83   KwaNdebele
.K85   Kwazulu
Cf. DT2400.Z85, Zululand

.L43   Lebowa
.L58   Little Karoo

.N36   Namaqualand (Little)

.P66   Pondoland
.Q83   QwaQwa

.T66   Tongaland
.T83   Transkei

.V45   Venda
.W58   Witwatersrand

.Z85   Zululand
Cf. DT2400.K85, Kwazulu

South Africa
 Local history and description - Continued
  Cities, towns, etc.
2403    Pretoria  (Table IV)
2405    Other cities, towns, etc., A-Z

        e. g.   .B56  Bloemfontein

              .C36  Cape Town (Table V)
              .D88  Durban (Table V)

              .E38  East London

              .J65  Johannesburg (Table V)
              .K56  Kimberley

              .P54  Pietermaritzburg
              .P68  Port Elizabeth

              .S68  Soweto


        BOTSWANA.   BECHUANALAND

2421    Periodicals.  Societies.  Serials
2428    Sources and documents
2434    Gazetteers.  Dictionaries, etc.
2435    Place names (General)
2436    Guidebooks
2437    General works
2439    General special
2441    Views
2446    Historic monuments, landmarks, scenery, etc. (General)
            For local, see DT2520+
2448    Description and travel
2450    Antiquities
            For local antiquities, see DT2520+
2452    Social life and customs.  Civilization.  Intellectual
          life
            For specific periods, see the period

~~South Africa~~
**Botswana. Bechuanaland** - Continued
Ethnography

|       |                                            |
|-------|--------------------------------------------|
| 2454  | General works                              |
| 2456  | Ethnic relations. Race relations           |
| 2458  | Individual elements in the population, A-Z  |

.G27   G/wi
.H36   Hambukushu

.K53   Kgatla

.P44   Pedi

.R75   Rolong
.S26   San
.S78   Sotho

.T35   Tannekwe
.T55   Tlhaping
.T89   Tswana

**History**

Periodicals. Societies. Serials, <u>see</u> DT2421

|       |                                                         |
|-------|---------------------------------------------------------|
| 2464  | Biography (Collective)                                  |
|       |     For individual biography, <u>see</u> the specific period |
|       | Historiography                                          |
| 2466  | General works                                           |
|       | Biography of historians, area studies specialists, archaeologists, etc. |
| 2467  | Collective                                              |
| 2468  | Individual, A-Z                                         |
| 2475  | General works                                           |
|       | General special                                         |
| 2478  | Political history                                       |
|       |     For specific periods, <u>see</u> the period |

|  | Botswana.  Bechuanaland |
|---|---|

Botswana.  Bechuanaland
 History - Continued
  By period
   Early to 1885
    Including conflicts with Transvaal and
    annexation of Rolong lands
    For Stellaland and Goshen, <u>see</u> DT2366
2483    General works
    Biography and memoirs
2485     Collective
2486     Individual, A-Z

     e. g. .S43 Sebitoane
        .S44 Sechele

2488    Difaqane, 1826-1851
     Including expansion of Bakololo
     Cf. DT1123, Mfecane.  Ngoni invasions
    1885-1966.  Bechuanaland Protectorate.  British
    Bechuanaland
     Including local activities of the British
     South Africa Company
     For works on the British South Africa Company
     in general, <u>see</u> DT2860; for Jameson Raid,
     <u>see</u> DT1889
2490    General works
    Biography and memoirs
2492     Collective
2493     Individual, A-Z

     e. g. .B37 Batheon
        .B38 Batheon II

        .K53 Khama, Tshekedi
        .K54 Khama III, Ngwato chief

        .S43 Sebele I
        .S45 Sekgoma

                **Botswana.   Bechuanaland**
                **History**
                    **By period** - Continued
                        1966-    . Independent

| | |
|---|---|
| 2496 | General works |
| | Biography and memoirs |
| 2498 | Collective |
| 2499 | Individual, A-Z |
| 2500 | Seretse Khama, 1966-1980 |
| |     Class here general works on life and administration |
| 2502 | Quett Masire, 1980- |
| |     Class here general works on life and administration |
| | Local history and description |
| 2520 | Provinces, regions, etc., A-Z |

                  e. g.   .K35   Kalahari Desert

                            .M35   Makgadikgadi Pans
                            .M65   Molopo River

                            .N53   Ngami, Lake
                            .O53   Okavango River and Swamp

                  Cities, towns, etc.

| | |
|---|---|
| 2523 | Gaborone |
| 2525 | Other cities, towns, etc., A-Z |

                  e. g.   .F83   Francistown

                            .K35   Kanye
                            .L73   Lobatse

                            .M36   Mahalapye
                            .M75   Molepolole

                            .S45   Selebi-Phikwe
                            .S47   Serowe

## LESOTHO. BASUTOLAND

| | |
|---|---|
| 2541 | Periodicals. Societies. Serials |
| 2549 | Sources and documents |
| 2554 | Gazetteers. Dictionaries, etc. |
| 2555 | Place names (General) |
| 2556 | Guidebooks |
| 2557 | General works |
| 2559 | General special |
| 2561 | Views |
| 2565 | Historic monuments, landmarks, scenery, etc. (General) |
| | For local, see DT2680+ |
| 2572 | Description and travel |
| 2580 | Antiquities |
| | For local antiquities, see DT2680+ |
| 2582 | Social life and customs. Civilization. Intellectual life |
| | For specific periods, see the period |
| | Ethnography |
| 2592 | General works |
| 2596 | Individual elements in the population, A-Z |
| | **History** |
| | Periodicals. Societies. Serials, see DT2541 |
| 2604 | Biography (Collective) |
| | For individual biography, see the specific period |
| | Historiography |
| 2606 | General works |
| | Biography of historians, area studies specialists, archaeologists, etc. |
| 2608 | Collective |
| 2609 | Individual, A-Z |
| 2615 | General works |
| | General special |
| 2618 | Political history |
| | For specific periods, see the period |
| | Foreign and general relations |
| | Class general works on the diplomatic history of a period with the period, e. g. DT2630. For works on relations with a specific country regardless of period, see DT2625 |
| 2623 | General works |
| 2625 | Relations with individual countries, A-Z |
| | For list of countries, see pp. 212-214 |

Lesotho.  Basutoland
  History - Continued
    By period
      Early to 1868
        Including claims by Orange Free State

| | |
|---|---|
| 2630 | General works |
| | Biography and memoirs |
| 2632 | Collective |
| 2634 | Individual, A-Z |

           e. g.   .M67  Moshoeshoe I

| | |
|---|---|
| 2636 | Wars with Orange Free State, 1865-1868 |
| | 1868-1966.  Basutoland.  British Protectorate |
| 2638 | General works |
| | Biography and memoirs |
| 2640 | Collective |
| 2642 | Individual, A-Z |

           e. g.   .G75  Griffith, Chief Nathaniel

                .M65  Mokhehle, Ntsu
                .M66  Moorosi

| | |
|---|---|
| 2644 | Cape rule, 1871-1884 |
| 2646 | Moorosi Rebellion, 1879 |
| 2648 | Gun War, 1880-1881 |
| | 1966-    .  Independent |
| 2652 | General works |
| | Biography and memoirs |
| 2654 | Collective |
| 2655 | Individual, A-Z |

           e. g.   .L45  Lekhanya, Justin

                .M65  Molapo, Charles
                .M67  Moshoeshoe II

| | |
|---|---|
| | 1966-1986.  Leabula Jonathan |
| 2657 | General works on life and administration |
| 2658 | South African raid on Maseru, 1982 |
| 2660 | 1986- |
| | Including January, 1986 Coup d'etat |

**Lesotho. Basutoland** - Continued
Local history and description
2680          Regions, districts, etc., A-Z

         e. g.    .M35   Malibamatso River
                 .M36   Maloti Mountains

       Cities, towns, etc.
2683         Maseru
2686         Other cities, towns, etc., A-Z

         e. g.    .B87   Butha-Buthe

                 .Q33   Qacha's Nek
                 .Q87   Quthing


## SWAZILAND

| | |
|---|---|
| 2701 | Periodicals. Societies. Serials |
| 2709 | Sources and documents |
| 2714 | Gazetteers. Dictionaries, etc. |
| 2715 | Place names (General) |
| 2717 | Guidebooks |
| 2719 | General works |
| 2721 | General special |
| 2723 | Views |
| 2725 | Historic monuments, landmarks, scenery, etc. (General) |
| |     For local, see DT2820+ |
| 2732 | Description and travel |
| 2740 | Antiquities |
| |     For local antiquities, see DT2820+ |
| 2742 | Social life and customs. Civilization. Intellectual life |
| |      For specific periods, see the period |
| | Ethnography |
| 2744 |    General works |
| 2746 |    Individual elements in the population, A-Z |

Swaziland - Continued
  **History**
    Periodicals. Societies. Serials, <u>see</u> DT2701
2754    Biography (Collective)
      For individual biography, <u>see</u> the specific
        period
    Historiography
2756     General works
     Biography of historians, area studies specialists,
       archaeologists, etc.
2757      Collective
2758      Individual, A-Z
2765   General works
   General special
2768    Political history
     For specific periods, <u>see</u> the period
    Foreign and general relations
     Class general works on the diplomatic history
      of a period with the period, e. g. DT2777+.
      For works on relations with a specific
      country regardless of period, <u>see</u> DT2775
2773     General works
2775     Relations with individual countries, A-Z
      For list of countries, <u>see</u> pp. 212-214
  **By period**
   To 1889
2777    General works
    Biography and memoirs
2779     Collective
2780     Individual, A-Z

      e.g.  .M33  Mbandzeni

          .M78  Mswati II, King of the Swazi

          .N58  Ngwane II

2782    Battle of Lubuya, 1854
2784    Battle at Sekhukhune's Stronghold, 1879
2786    Convention of Pretoria, 1881

                    Swaziland
                      History
                        By period - Continued
                          1889-1968.  British rule
2788                          General works
                              Biography and memoirs
2790                              Collective
2791                              Individual, A-Z

                                      e. g.   .B58  Bhunu

2793                          Transvaal rule, 1894-1902
2795                          Land partition, 1907

                          1968-     .  Independent
2797                          General works
                              Biography and memoirs
2799                              Collective
2800                              Individual, A-Z

                                      e. g.   .D53  Dhlamini, Mabandla

                                              .D54  Dhlamini, Mfanasibili

                                              .D94  Dzeliwe, Queen Regent

                                              .M85  Msibi, George
                                              .N86  Ntombi, Queen Regent

2802                          1968-1982.  Sobhuza II
                                  Class here general works on the life and
                                      reign
2804                          1982-1986.  Interregnum
2806                          1986-     .  Mswati III
                                  Class here general works on the life and
                                      reign

Swaziland - Continued
Local history and description
2820        Regions, districts, etc., A-Z

e. g.    .H56   Hhohho

.L43   Lebombo Plateau

.S55   Shisilweni

Cities, towns, etc.
2823        Mbanane
2825        Other cities, towns, etc., A-Z

e. g.    .B86   Bunya

.K84   Kwaluseni

.M35   Manzini.   Bremersdorp

.S58   Siteki

## BRITISH CENTRAL AFRICA.
## FEDERATION OF RHODESIA AND NYASALAND

Including works on Malawi, Zambia and Zimbabwe
treated together.  For Malawi (Nyasaland) alone,
see DT3161+.  For Zambia (Northern Rhodesia)
alone, see DT3031+.  For Zimbabwe (Southern
Rhodesia) alone, see DT2871+

| | |
|---|---|
| 2831 | Periodicals.  Societies.  Serials |
| 2839 | Sources and documents |
| 2844 | General works |
| 2851 | General special |
| 2856 | Description and travel |

**History**
   Periodicals.  Societies.  Serials, see DT2831
   Biography (Collective), see DT2914

| | |
|---|---|
| 2858 | General works |

**By period**
   Early to 1890, see DT2937

| | |
|---|---|
| 2860 | 1890-1923 |
| | Including general works on the British South Africa Company.  For activities of the Company in specific countries, see the country |
| 2862 | 1923-1953.  British Protectorates |
| 2864 | 1953-1964.  Federation of Rhodesia and Nyasaland |

## ZIMBABWE.   SOUTHERN RHODESIA

| | |
|---|---|
| 2871 | Periodicals. Societies. Serials |
| 2879 | Sources and documents |
| 2884 | Gazetteers. Dictionaries, etc. |
| 2885 | Place names (General) |
| 2886 | Guidebooks |
| 2889 | General works |
| 2891 | General special |
| 2893 | Views |
| | Historic monuments, landmarks, scenery, etc. (General) |
| |     For local, see DT3020+ |
| 2895 |   General works |
| 2897 |   Preservation |
| | Description and travel |
| 2900 |   Early to 1965 |
| 2902 |   1965-1982 |
| 2904 |   1983- |
| 2906 | Antiquities |
| |     For local antiquities, see DT3020+ |
| 2908 | Social life and customs. Civilization. Intellectual life |
| |     For specific periods, see the period |
| | Ethnography |
| 2910 |   General works |
| 2912 |   Ethnic and race relations |
| 2913 |   Individual elements in the population, A-Z |

        .B38   Barwe
        .B85   British

        .C75   Colored people

        .E38   East Indians
        .E87   Europeans

        .G68   Gova

        .K38   Karanga
        .K53   Kgatla

**Zimbabwe.   Southern Rhodesia**

Ethnography

2913          Individual elements in the population, A-Z - Continued

          .M38   Mashona
          .N44   Ndebele

          .P44   Pedi

          .T36   Tangwena
          .T38   Tawara

          .T55   Tlhaping
          .T78   Tswana

          .Z49   Zezuru

**History**

         Periodicals.   Societies.   Serials, see DT2871

2914          Biography (Collective)

           For individual biography, see the specific
             period

         Historiography

2916           General works

          Biography of historians, area studies specialists,
            archaeologists, etc.

2917             Collective
2918             Individual, A-Z
2925        General works

       General special

2928          Political history

           For specific periods, see the period

         Foreign and general relations

           Class general works on the diplomatic history
             of a period with the period, e. g. DT2937+.
             For works on relations with a specific
             country regardless of period, see DT2935

2933          General works
2935          Relations with individual countries, A-Z

           For list of countries, see pp. 212-214

                  **Zimbabwe.   Southern Rhodesia**
                    **History** - Continued
                        **By period**
                            Early to 1890

2937                               General works
                              Biography and memoirs
2939                                 Collective
2940                                 Individual, A-Z

                                        e. g.   .D66   Dombo, King of Changamire

                                                .K35   Kaliphi
                                                .L73   Lobengula

                                                .M38   Matope
                                                .M39   Mavura
                                                .M95   Mzilikazi

                              Monomotapa, ca. 1000-ca. 1700
2942                               General works
2943                               Expedition of Antonio Fernandez, 1512-1514
                              Barreto Expedition, 1572, <u>see</u> DT3355
                              Dombo's Expedition against the Portuguese,
                                  1593, <u>see</u> DT3359
2945                               Expedition against Kuparavidze, 1632
2947                            Rozwi Empire, ca. 1700-1834
2949                            Sack of Great Zimbabwe by Zwangendaba's
                             Ngoni, 1835
                                Cf. DT1123, Mfecane.   Ngoni invasions
2951                            Ndebele Invasions, 1838-1839
2953                            Patterson Expedition, 1878
2955                            Moffat Treaty, 1888
2957                            Rudd Concession, 1888
                        1890-1923.   British South African Company
                        administration
                            Cf. DT2860, British South Africa Company
2959                         General works
                        Biography and memoirs
2961                           Collective
2963                           Individual, A-Z

                                        e. g.   .M64   Moffat, John

                                                .S45   Selous, Frederick

Zimbabwe.   Southern Rhodesia
  History
    By period
      1890-1923.   British South Africa Company
          administration - Continued

|        |                                               |
|--------|-----------------------------------------------|
| 2964   | Pioneer Column, 1890                          |
| 2966   | Ndebele War, 1893                             |
| 2968   | Ndebele War.  First Chimurenga, 1896-1897 |
| 2970   | Shona Uprising, 1896                          |

      1923-1953.   British Crown colony

| 2972 | General works |
|------|---------------|
|      | Biography and memoirs |
| 2974 | Collective |
| 2975 | Individual, A-Z |

             e. g.   .C65   Coghlan, Charles

                     .H85   Huggins, Godfrey

                     .M64   Moffat, Howard

      1953-1965
        Cf. DT2864, Federation of Rhodesia and
           Nyasaland

| 2976 | General works |
|------|---------------|
|      | Biography and memoirs |
| 2978 | Collective |
| 2979 | Individual, A-Z |

             e. g.   .C55   Chikerema, James

                     .N93   Nyandoro, George

Zimbabwe.   Southern Rhodesia
    History
        By period - Continued
            1965-1980
2981            General works
                Biography and memoirs
2983                Collective
2984                Individual, A-Z

                        e. g.   .M89  Muzorewa, Abel

                                .N56  Nkomo, Joshua

                                .S58  Sithole, Ndabaningi
                                .S65  Smith, Ian

2986            Unilateral Declaration of Independence (UDI),
                    1965
*1766-1980* 1972-1979.  War of National Liberation.  Second
                    Chimurenga
2988            General works
2990            Personal narratives
2992            Individual events, battles, etc., A-Z
2994            1979-1980.  Transitional government.  Lancaster
                    House Conference
            1980-    .  Independent
2996            General works
                Biography and memoirs
2998                Collective
2999                Individual, A-Z
3000            Mugabe, Robert, 1980-
                    Class here general works on life and
                        administration
        Local history and description
3020        Regions, districts, etc., A-Z

                        e. g.   .K38  Kariba, Lake

                                .M35  Manicaland
                                .M37  Mashonaland
                                .M38  Matabeleland
                                .M39  Matopo Hills

Zimbabwe.  Southern Rhodesia
  Local history and description - Continued
    Cities, towns, etc.

3022       Harare.  Salisbury
3025       Other cities, towns, etc., A-Z

e. g.  .C54  Chegutu.  Hartley
      .C55  Chinhoyi.  Chipinga
      .C56  Chivhu.  Enkeldoorn

      .E85  Esigodini.  Essexdale

      .G84  Great Zimbabwe
      .G87  Guruwe.  Sipolilo
      .G89  Gweru.  Gwelo

      .H93  Hwange.  Wankie

      .K34  Kadoma.  Gatooma
      .K84  Kwekwe.  Que Que

      .M37  Masvingo.  Fort Victoria
      .M43  Mbalabala.  Balla Balla

      .M86  Mutare.  Umtali
      .M88  Mvuma.  Umvuma
      .M94  Mwenezi.  Nuanetsi

      .N83  Nuazira.  Inyazura

      .S36  Sango.  Vila Salazar
      .S58  Shurugwe.  Selukwe

      .T85  Tsholotsho.  Tjolotjo

      .Z95  Zvishavane.  Shabani

## ZAMBIA. NORTHERN RHODESIA

| | |
|---|---|
| 3031 | Periodicals. Societies. Serials |
| 3035 | Sources and documents |
| 3037 | Gazetteers. Dictionaries, etc. |
| 3039 | Place names (General) |
| 3041 | Guidebooks |
| 3042 | General works |
| 3044 | General special |
| 3046 | Views |
| 3048 | Historic monuments, landmarks, scenery, etc. (General) |
| |     For local, see DT3140+ |
| 3050 | Description and travel |
| 3051 | Antiquities |
| |     For local antiquities, see DT3140+ |
| 3052 | Social life and customs. Civilization. Intellectual life |
| |     For specific periods, see the period |
| | Ethnography |
| 3054 |   General works |
| 3056 |   Ethnic and race relations |
| 3058 |   Individual elements in the population, A-Z |

          .A63  Ambo
          .B46  Bemba
          .B58  Bisa
          .C53  Chewa
          .C56  Chokwe

          .E38  East Indians
          .E87  Europeans

          .F56  Fipa
          .G79  Gova

          .I53  Ila

          .K36  Kaonde
          .K93  Kwangwa

Zambia.  Northern Rhodesia
    Ethnography
3058        Individual elements in the population, A-Z - Continued

          .L35  Lala
          .L36  Lamba
          .L46  Lenje

          .L69  Lozi
          .L89  Luvale

          .M35  Mambwe
          .M38  Mbunda
          .N44  Ndembu
          .N53  Ngangela
          .N56  Nkoya
          .N93  Nyanja

          .T48  Thonga
          .T65  Tonga
          .U65  Unga
          .U85  Ushi

          .Y66  Yombe

**History**
    Periodicals.  Societies.  Serials, see DT3031
3064        Biography (Collective)
          For individual biography, see the specific
            period
    Historiography
3066         General works
      Biography of historians, area studies specialists,
          archaeologists, etc.
3068         Collective
3069         Individual, A-Z
3071    General works

Zambia.  Northern Rhodesia
   History - Continued
     General special
3073       Political history
         For specific periods, see the period
       Foreign and general relations
         Class general works on the diplomatic history
           of a period with the period, e. g. DT3079+.
           For works on relations with a specific
           country regardless of period, see DT3077
3075       General works
3077       Relations with individual countries, A-Z
         For list of countries, see pp. 212-214
   **By period**
     Early to 1890
3079       General works
       Biography and memoirs
3080        Collective
3081        Individual, A-Z

          e. g.   .K35  Kanyemba, Jose do Rosario
                     Andrade
               .K38  Kazembe III Lukwesa
               .K39  Kazembe IV Keleka

               .L48  Lewanika
               .M64  Mpenzeni

               .S43  Sebituane
               .S56  Sipopa

               .W48  Westbeech, George

3083        Expedition of Monteiro and Gamitto, 1831
3085        Arab and Swahili Expeditions, ca. 1840-ca. 1860
3087        Ngoni Invasions, ca. 1840-1880.  Mfecane
          Cf. DT1123, Mfecane.  Ngoni invasions
3089        Ndebele Invasions, ca. 1860-ca. 1880

```
                    Zambia.  Northern Rhodesia
                      History
                        By period - Continued
                          1890-1924.  British South Africa Company
                            administration
                              For Ware Concession and British South Africa
                                Company attempts to annex Katanga (Shaba),
                                see DT665.K3
                              For general works on British South Africa
                                Company, see DT2860
         3091                   General works
                                Biography and memoirs
         3093                     Collective
         3094                     Individual, A-Z
         3097                   Gwembe Tonga Uprising, 1909
         3099                   Lunda Uprising, 1912
         3101                   Luvale Uprising, 1923
                          1924-1953.  British Protectorate
         3103                   General works
                                Biography and memoirs
         3105                     Collective
         3106                     Individual, A-Z

                                    e. g.   .G78  Gore-Browne, Steward

                                            .Y35  Yamba, Dauti

                          1953-1964
                              Cf. DT2864, Federation of Rhodesia and
                                    Nyasaland
         3108                   General works
                                Biography and memoirs
         3110                     Collective
         3111                     Individual, A-Z

                                    e. g.   .N58  Nkumbula, Harry

                                            .W45  Welensky, Roy
```

          **Zambia. Northern Rhodesia**
            **History**
               **By period** - Continued
                  1964-    . Independent
                       For Lumpa Church Rebellion, 1964, <u>see</u>
                          BR1453.Z3
                       For raids of ZANU installations in Zambia,
                          <u>see</u> DT2988+

3113                    General works
                    Biography and memoirs
3115                      Collective
3117                      Individual, A-Z

                           e. g.   .K36  Kapwepwe, Simon

3119                    Kenneth Kaunda, 1964-
                      Class here general works on life and
                       administration

         **Local history and description**
3140                  Provinces, regions, etc., A-Z

                         e. g.    .B36  Bangweulu Lake and Swamp

                                 .C66  Copperbelt

                                 .K35  Kafue Flats

                                 .M84  Muchinga Mountains

                                 .V54  Victoria Falls

                                 .W48  Western Province.  Barotseland

Zambia.  Northern Rhodesia
Local history and description - Continued
Cities, towns, etc.

| | |
|---|---|
| 3142 | Lusaka |
| 3145 | Other cities, towns, etc., A-Z |

e. g.    .C55   Chilialombwe
.C56   Chingola

.K33   Kabwe
.K58   Kitwe

.L58   Livingstone
.L83   Luanshya

.M85   Mufulira

.N46   Ndola

## MALAWI.  NYASALAND

| | |
|---|---|
| 3161 | Periodicals.  Societies.  Serials |
| 3167 | Sources and documents |
| 3169 | Gazetteers.  Dictionaries, etc. |
| 3171 | Place names (General) |
| 3173 | Guidebooks |
| 3174 | General works |
| 3176 | General special |
| 3178 | Views |
| 3180 | Historic monuments, landmarks, scenery, etc. (General)<br>For local, see DT3252+ |
| 3182 | Description and travel |
| 3185 | Antiquities<br>For local antiquities, see DT3252+ |
| 3187 | Social life and customs.  Civilization.  Intellectual life<br>For specific periods, see the period |

Malawi. Nyasaland - Continued
    Ethnography
3189      General works
3190      Ethnic and race relations
3192      Individual elements in the population, A-Z

        .C54  Chewa

        .L66  Lomwe

        .M35  Manganja

        .N44  Ngoni
        .N56  Nkhonde
        .N83  Nyanja

        .T48  Thonga
        .T85  Tumbuka

        .Y36  Yao

**History**
    Periodicals. Societies. Serials, see DT3161
3194    Biography (Collective)
      For individual biography, see the specific
        period
    Historiography
3196      General works
      Biography of historians, area studies specialists,
        archaeologists, etc.
3198        Collective
3199        Individual, A-Z
3201    General works
    General special
3204      Political history
        For specific periods, see the period

       **Malawi. Nyasaland**
        **History**
           General special - Continued
            Foreign and general relations
              Class general works on the diplomatic history
                of a period with the period, e. g. DT3211+.
                For works on relations with a specific
                country regardless of period, <u>see</u> DT3208

|  |  |
|---|---|
| 3206 | General works |
| 3208 | Relations with individual countries, A-Z |

              For list of countries, <u>see</u> pp. 212-214
          **By period**
            To 1891
              Including Livingstonia Central Africa
                Company, African Lakes Company and
                Portuguese claims
              Cf. DT2860, British South Africa Company
                claims on Mozambique and Nyasaland

|  |  |
|---|---|
| 3211 | General works |
|  | Biography and memoirs |
| 3213 |    Collective |
| 3214 |    Individual, A-Z |

                 e. g.   .M65  Moir, Frederick
                          .M66  Moir, John

                          .M85   Mulambwa

            1891-1953
              Including British Central Africa Protectorate
                 and Nyasaland Protectorate
              For British Central Africa, <u>see</u> DT2860+

|  |  |
|---|---|
| 3216 | General works |
|  | Biography and memoirs |
| 3218 |    Collective |
| 3219 |    Individual, A-Z |

                 e. g.   .C55  Chilembwe, John

                         .M56  Mlozi
                         .M85  Mumba, Levi

                         .S53  Sharpe, Alfred

                **Malawi. Nyasaland**
                  **History**
                    **By period**

|      |      |
|------|------|
|      | 1891-1953 - Continued |
| 3221 | Campaign against Mlozi, 1887-1895 |
| 3223 | Mpenzeni War, 1898 |
| 3225 | Chilembwe Rebellion, 1915 |
|      | 1953-1964 |
|      | Cf. DT2864, Federation of Rhodesia and Nyasaland |
| 3227 | General works |
|      | Biography and memoirs |
| 3229 | Collective |
| 3230 | Individual, A-Z |
|      | 1964- . Independent |
| 3232 | General works |
|      | Biography and memoirs |
| 3234 | Collective |
| 3235 | Individual, A-Z |
|      | e. g. .C55 Chipembere, Masauko |
|      | .T46 Tembo, John |
| 3236 | Hastings Kamuzu Banda, 1964- |
|      | Class here general works on the life and administration |
| 3237 | Chipembere Rebellion, 1965 |

**Local history and description**

| 3252 | Regions, districts, etc., A-Z |
|------|------|
|      | e. g. .M35 Malawi, Lake (Lake Nyasa) |
|      | .M85 Mulanje Mountains |
|      | .S55 Shire River and Valley |
|      | .Z65 Zomba Plateau |

Malawi.  Nyasaland
  **Local history and description** - Continued
    Cities, towns, etc.
3254        Lilongwe
3257        Other cities, towns, etc., A-Z

                e. g.   .B53   Blantyre

                        .L56   Limbe

                        .M98   Mzuzu

                        .Z66   Zomba


### MOZAMBIQUE

3291        Periodicals.  Societies.  Serials
3293        Sources and documents
3294        Gazetteers.  Dictionaries, etc.
3295        Place names (General)
3297        Guidebooks
3299        General works
3301        General special
3302        Views
3305        Historic monuments, landmarks, scenery, etc. (General)
                For local, see DT3410
            Description and travel
3308          Early through 1800
3310          1801-1980
3312          1981-
3318        Antiquities
                For local antiquities, see DT3410
3320        Social life and customs.  Civilization.  Intellectual
              life
                For specific periods, see the period

Mozambique - Continued
Ethnography
3324            General works
3326            Ethnic and race relations
3328            Individual elements in the population, A-Z

                .B33   Ba-Ronga
                .B37   Barwe
                .C67   Chopi

                .G73   Goans

                .L66   Lomwe

                .M35   Makonde
                .M36   Makua

                .N58   Nguni
                .N93   Nyanja

                .P68   Portuguese
                .R83   Rue
                .T38   Tarawa
                .T48   Thonga

                .V35   Valenge

                .Y36   Yao


**History**
        Periodicals.  Societies.  Serials, <u>see</u> DT3291
3330        Biography (Collective)
                For individual biography, <u>see</u> the specific
                  period
        Historiography
3332        General works
            Biography of historians, area studies specialists,
                archaeologists, etc.
3334            Collective
3335            Individual, A-Z
3337    General works

```
                    Mozambique
                      History - Continued
                        General special
      3339                  Political history
                              For specific periods, see the period
                            Foreign and general relations
                              Class general works on the diplomatic
                                history of a period with the period,
                                e. g. DT3354+.  For works on relations
                                with a specific country regardless of
                                period, see DT3343
      3341                    General works
      3343                    Relations with individual countries, A-Z
                                For list of countries, see pp. 212-214

                        By period
                          Early to 1505
                            Including Arab and East Indian domination
      3345                    General works
                            Biography and memoirs
      3347                      Collective
      3348                      Individual, A-Z
                          1505-1698
                            Including the Captaincy of Sofala
      3350                    General works
                            Biography and memoirs
      3352                      Collective
      3353                      Individual, A-Z

                                    e. g.   .B38  Barreto, Francisco

      3355                  Barreto expedition, 1572
      3357                  Dutch expedition, 1604
      3359                  Expedition of Dombo of the Changamire,
                              1692-1695
                                Cf. DT2942, Monomotapa
```

Mozambique
  History
    **By period** - Continued
      1698-1891
        Including border disputes with Nyasaland
          and claims of the British South Africa
          Company.
        For general works on the British South
          Africa Company, <u>see</u> DT2860

| | |
|---|---|
| 3361 | General works |
| | Biography and memoirs |
| 3363 |   Collective |
| 3364 |   Individual, A-Z |

            e. g.  .B66  Bonga

                .G68  Gouveia, Manuel Antonio de
                      Sousa
                .G86  Gungunhana

                .M89  Muzila

                .S5  Shangana

| | |
|---|---|
| 3366 | Mfecane.  Ngoni invasions, ca. 1820-ca. 1850 |
| |   Cf. DT1123, Mfecane.  Ngoni invasions |
| |     (Southern Africa) |
| 3368 | Zulu conquest of Lourenco Marques, 1833 |
| 3370 | Attack of Sofala, 1836 |
| 3372 | Attack of Inhambane, 1843 |
| 3374 | Fall of Massangano, 1888 |
| | 1891-1975 |
| |   Including activities of the Companhia de |
| |     Mocambique and the Companhia do Niassa |
| 3376 | General works |
| | Biography and memoirs |
| 3378 |   Collective |
| 3379 |   Individual, A-Z |

            e. g.  .M66  Mondlane, Eduardo

Mozambique
  History
    By period
      1891-1975 - Continued

| | |
|---|---|
| 3381 | War with Shangaan, 1894-1895 |
| 3383 | Campaigns in interior, 1885-1912 |
| 3385 | Zambezi Rebellion, 1917 |
| 3387 | National liberation struggle, 1964-1975 |

      1975-   . Independent
        For raids against ZAPU and ZANU forces in
          Mozambique, see DT2988+

| | |
|---|---|
| 3389 | General works |
| | Biography and memoirs |
| 3391 | Collective |
| 3392 | Individual, A-Z |

      1975-1986

| | |
|---|---|
| 3393 | Samora Machel, 1975-1986 |

        Class here general works on the life and
          administration

| | |
|---|---|
| 3394 | 1976-   . Insurgency movement (RNM) |
| 3396 | Nkomati Accord, 1984 |
| 3398 | Joaquim Chissano, 1986- |

        Class here general works on the life and
          administration

**Local history and description**

| | |
|---|---|
| 3410 | Provinces, districts, regions, etc., A-Z |

        e. g.   .C36  Cahora Bassa.  Cabora Bassa

              .G39  Gaza
              .I65  Inhambane

              .M36  Manica.  Vila Pery
              .M37  Manjacaze.  Muchopes
              .M38  Maputo Province.  Lourenço Marques

              .N36  Nampula.  Moçambique
              .N53 Niassa

              .S65  Sofala.  Beira
              .T48  Tete

              .Z36  Zambia

**Mozambique**
   **Local history and description** - Continued
      Cities, towns, etc.

| | |
|---|---|
| 3412 | Maputo. Lourenco Marques  (Table IV |
| 3415 | Other cities, towns, etc., A-Z |

e. g.   .A65   Angoche.  António Enes

.B45   Beira

.C36   Cantandica.  Vila Gouveia

.C54   Chicualacuala.  Malvernia
.C55   Chilembene.  Aldeia da Madragoa
.C56   Chimoio.  Vila Pery
.C58   Chokwe.  Trigo de Morais

.C83   Cuamba.  Nova Freixo

.G85   Guija.  Vila Alferes Chamusca

.L53   Lichinga.  Vila Cabral
.L87   Lupichili.  Olivenca

.M33   Macaloge.  Miranda
.M35   Mahlazene.  Santa Comba
.M38   Matola.  Vila Salazar

.P45   Pemba.  Porto Amelia

.X35   Xai-Xai.  João Belo

| | | |
|---|---|---|
| 1 | | Periodicals. Societies. Serials |
| 4 | | Biography (Collective) |
| 10 | | Gazetteers. Dictionaries, etc. |
| 15 | | Guidebooks |
| 17 | | General works |
| 18 | | General special |
| | | South Sea description and travel. Voyages |
| 19 | |   General history of voyages and discoveries |
| 20 | |   Through 1800 |
| 21 | |   1801-1897 |
| 22 | |   1898-1950 |
| 23 | |   1951-1980 |
| | .5 |   1981- |
| 28 | | Social life and customs. Social antiquities. Ethnography |
| | |     Cf. GN662+, Anthropology |

**History**

| | | |
|---|---|---|
| | | Historiography |
| | .11 |   General works |
| | |   Biography of historians, area studies specialists, |
| | |      archaeologists, etc. |
| | .12 |     Collective |
| | .13 |     Individual, A-Z |
| | | Study and teaching |
| | .2 |   General works |
| | .25 |   By region or country, A-Z |
| | |     Subarranged by author |
| | .3 | General works |
| | .35 | Political and diplomatic history. Control of the |
| | |   Pacific. Colonies and possessions |
| | |     Cf. DS510.7+, Far Eastern question |
| 29 | |   General works |
| | |   By country |
| 30 | |     United States |
| 32 | |     Canada |
| 40 | |     Great Britain |
| 50 | |     France |
| 60 | |     Germany |
| 65 | |     Spain |
| 66 | |     Japan |

## AUSTRALIA

| | |
|---|---|
| 80 | Periodicals.  Sources and documents.  Collections.  Yearbooks |
| 82 | Biography (Collective) |
| 90 | Gazetteers.  Dictionaries, etc. |
| 91 | Place names (General) |
| 93 | Monumental and picturesque |
| 94 | Preservation |
| 95 | Guidebooks.  Descriptive handbooks, etc. |
| 96 | General works |
| .5 | Historical geography |
| | Description and travel |
| 97 | History of travel |
| | To 1788 |
| 98 | Personal narratives |
| .1 | General works |
| 99 | 1788-1836 |
| 101 | 1837-1850 |
| | 1851-1900 |
| 102 | General works |
| 103 | Gold discovery, 1851 |
| 104 | 1901-1950 |
| 105 | 1951-1980 |
| .2 | 1981- |
| 106 | Antiquities |
| 107 | Social life and customs.  Civilization.  Intellectual life |

**History**

| | |
|---|---|
| | Historiography |
| 108 | General works |
| | Biography of historians |
| 109.A2A-Z | Collective |
| .A3-Z | Individual, A-Z |
| .5 | Study and teaching |
| 110 | General works |
| .5 | Comic and satiric works |
| 112 | Compends |

**Australia**

  **History** - Continued

    General special

112.3        Military history

    .4        Naval history

         Diplomatic history. Foreign and general relations

           Class general works on the diplomatic history of a period with the period, e. g. DU114+. For works on relations with a specific country regardless of period, see DU113.5

113        General works

    .5        Relations with individual countries, A-Z

           For list of countries, see pp. 212-214

  **By period**

       To 1788, see DU98.1

       1788-1900

114        Sources and documents

115        General works

    .2        Biography and memoirs

          .A2A-Z   Collective

          .A3-Z    Individual, A-Z

       1900-1945

116        General works

    .18        Foreign and general relations

    .2        Biography and memoirs

          .A2A-Z   Collective

          .A3-Z    Individual, A-Z

       1945-

    .9        Sources and documents

117        General works

    .13        Addresses, essays, lectures

    .14        Social life and customs. Civilization. Intellectual life

    .15        Military history

    .17        Political history

    .18        Foreign and general relations

         Biography and memoirs

    .19          Collective

    .2          Individual, A-Z

        **Australia** - Continued
         Ethnography
           Cf. GN665+, Anthropology

120          General works
122          Individual elements in the population, A-Z
              Afghans, see .P87
        .A5    Americans
        .A7    Armenians

        .B34   Balts
        .B7    British
               Including Cornish

        .C5    Chinese
             Cornish, see .B7
        .C7    Croats

        .D8    Dutch

        .E17   East Indians
             English, see .B7
        .E8    Estonians

        .F55   Finns
        .F73   French

        .G4    Germans
        .G7    Greeks

        .H8    Hungarians

        .I53   Indochinese
        .I7    Irish
        .I8    Italians

        .L3    Latvians
        .L42   Lebanese
        .L5    Lithuanians

        .M3    Macedonians
        .M34   Maltese

**Australia**
Ethnography
122        Individual elements in the population, A-Z - Continued

.N67    Norwegians
.P6     Poles
.P87    Pushtuns

.R8     Russians

.S3     Scandinavians
.S4     Scotch
.S67    Sorbs
.S73    Spaniards
.S94    Swedes
.S95    Swiss

.U4     Ukrainians
.V53    Vietnamese

.Y8     Yugoslavs (General)

125        Australian aborigines.  By group, A-Z

.A49    Alyawara

.B35    Bindubi
.B67    Burera

.D35    Dangadi
.D59    Diyari

.G33    Gadjerong
.G8     Gurundji

.J55    Jiman

.K3     Kaurna
.K77    Kurnai

.L37    Lardil

**Australia**
Ethnography
125      Australian aborigines.  By group, A-Z - Continued

.M29    Mandjildjara
.M33    Maung
.M8     Murngin
.M83    Muruwari

.N36    Narangga
.N37    Narrinyeri
.N94    Nunggubuyu
.N97    Nyunga

.P44    Pibelmen
.P48    Pintubi
.P5     Pitjandjara

.T5     Tiwi
.T67    Torres Strait Islanders

.W27    Wailpi
.W3     Walbiri
.W5     Wiradjuri
.W58    Wonnarua
.W6     Worora
.W8     Wunambal
.W87    Wurundjeri

.Y33    Yaburara
.Y35    Yangura

|   |   |
|---|---|
| | **Australia** - Continued |
| 135 | Other |
| 145 | Australian Capital Territory.  Canberra |
| | **New South Wales** |
| 150 | Periodicals.  Societies.  Serials.  Yearbooks |
| 155 | Gazetteers.  Handbooks |
| | General works.  Description and travel |
| 160 | Through 1836 |
| 161 | 1837-1950 |
| 162 | 1951- |
| | **History** |
| 170 | General and early |
| 172 | Biography and memoirs |

        .A2A-Z  Collective
        .A3-Z   Individual, A-Z

          .M3   Macquarie, Lachlan

          .P2   Parkes, Sir Henry
          .P58  Phillip, Arthur

          .S77  Strzelecki, Sir Paul Edmund de

|   |   |
|---|---|
| 177 | Other |
| | **Local history and description** |
| 178 | Sydney |
| 180 | Other cities, regions, etc., A-Z |

     e. g.  .A8   Australian Alps

          .B56  Blue Mountains
          .B8   Broken Hill

          .F6   Forbes
          .K7   Kosciusko, Mount

          .M8   Murray River and Valley

          .N5   New Italy (Colony)
          .N56  Newcastle
          .N6   Norfolk Island

          .W3   Wagga Wagga

                          **Australia** - Continued
                             **Victoria**
200                              Periodicals.  Societies.  Serials.  Yearbooks
205                              Gazetteers.  Handbooks.  Directories
                                 General works.  Description and travel
210                                  Through 1850
212                                  1851-1950
213                                  1951-

                             **History**
220                              General and early
222                              Biography and memoirs
                                     .A2A-Z  Collective
                                     .A3-Z   Individual, A-Z

                                         .B8  Buckley, William

                                         .K4  Kelly, Edward
                                         .L3  Lalor, Peter

                                         .R8  Russel, George

                                         .S8  Swinburne, George

227                              Other
                             **Local history and description**
228                              Melbourne (Table IV)[1]
230                              Other cities, regions, etc., A-Z

                                     e. g.  .B3  Ballarat

                                            .B4  Bendigo

                                            .G4  Geelong

—————————

[1] For subarrangement, <u>see</u> Tables, p. 216

|       | Australia - Continued |
|-------|------------------------|
|       | **Queensland** |
| 250   | Periodicals.  Societies.  Serials.  Yearbooks |
| 255   | Gazetteers.  Handbooks |
| 260   | General works.  Description and travel |
|       | **History** |
| 270   | General and early |
| 272   | Biography and memoirs |

.A2A-Z  Collective
.A3-Z   Individual, A-Z

.K34  Kennedy, Alexander

|       |                        |
|-------|------------------------|
| 274   | Ethnography |
| 277   | Other |
|       | **Local history and description** |
| 278   | Brisbane |
| 280   | Other cities, regions, etc., A-Z |

e. g.  .C25  Cairns
       .C3   Cape York Peninsula

       .D2   Darling Downs
       .D7   Dunk Island

       .G5   Gladstone

       .M22  McPherson Range
       .M7   Moreton Bay

       .T7   Torres Strait

       .W4   Wellesley Islands

|     | Australia - Continued |
|-----|-----|
|     | **South Australia** |
| 300 | Periodicals. Societies. Serials. Yearbooks |
| 305 | Gazetteers. Handbooks |
| 310 | General works. Description and travel |
|     | **History** |
| 320 | General and early |
| 322 | Biography and memoirs |
|     | .A2A-Z  Collective |
|     | .A3-Z   Individual, A-Z |
|     | .A5  Angas, George Fife |
|     | .F5  Fisher, Sir James Hurtle |
|     | .L6  Light, William |
| 325 | Ethnography |
| 327 | Other |
|     | **Local history and description** |
| 328 | Adelaide |
| 330 | Other cities, regions, etc., A-Z |
|     | e. g.  .B3  Barmera |
|     | .E5  Encounter Bay |
|     | .E9  Eyre Peninsula |
|     | .G8  Gumeracha |
|     | **Western Australia** |
| 350 | Periodicals. Societies. Serials. Yearbooks |
|     | Museums, exhibitions, etc. |
| 351 | General works |
| .2  | By place, A-Z |
|     | Subarranged by author |
| 355 | Gazetteers. Handbooks |
| 360 | General works. Description and travel |

**Australia**
**Western Australia** - Continued
  **History**
370      General and early
372      Biography and memoirs
      .A2A-Z   Collective
      .A3-Z    Individual, A-Z

        .G3    Gaston, Albert

        .H34   Harris, Charles M.

        .K5    Kirwan, Sir John

374      Ethnography
377      Other
  **Local history and description**
378      Perth
380      Other cities, regions, etc., A-Z

       e. g.   .F8     Fremantle

           .K5     Kimberley

           .N4     Nursia (Norcia)

           .R68    Rottnest Island

390      Central Australia
391      Northern Australia
       Class here works dealing collectively with the
         Northern territory and the northern parts
         of Queensland and Western Australia
  **Northern Territory of Australia**
392      Periodicals.   Serials.   Yearbooks
394      Gazetteers.   Handbooks.   Guidebooks
395      General works.   Description and travel
    **History**
396      General works
397      Biography and memoirs
      .A2A-Z   Collective
      .A3-Z    Individual, A-Z

**Australia**
  **Northern Territory of Australia** - Continued

| | |
|---|---|
| 397.5 | Ethnography |
| 398 | Regions, cities, etc., A-Z |

        e. g.  .A7  Arnhem Land

              .D3  Darwin

**New Zealand**

| | |
|---|---|
| 400 | Periodicals.  Societies.  Serials.  Yearbooks |
| 405 | Gazetteers.  Handbooks |
| .5 | Guidebooks |
| 406 | Monumental and picturesque |
| 408 | General works |
| | Description and travel |
| 409 | History of travel |
| 410 | Through 1839 |
| 411 | 1840-1950 |
| 412 | 1951-1980 |
| 413 | 1981- |
| 416 | Antiquities |
| 418 | Social life and customs.  Civilization. |
| | Intellectual life |
| | **History** |
| | Historiography |
| 419 | General works |
| | Biography of historians |
| .2 | Collective |
| .3 | Individual, A-Z |
| 420 | General works |
| | To 1840 |
| .12 | General works |
| | Biography and memoirs |
| .13 | Collective |
| .14 | Individual, A-Z |
| | 1840-1876 |
| .16 | General works |
| | Biography and memoirs |
| .17 | Collective |
| .18 | Individual, A-Z |

New Zealand
  History - Continued
    1876-1918

|||
|---|---|
| 420.22 | General works |
| | Biography and memoirs |
| .23 | Collective |
| .24 | Individual, A-Z |
| | 1918-1945 |
| .26 | General works |
| | Biography and memoirs |
| .27 | Collective |
| .28 | Individual, A-Z |
| | 1945- |
| .32 | General works |
| | Biography and memoirs |
| .33 | Collective |
| .34 | Individual, A-Z |
| .5 | Military history |
| | Political and diplomatic history. Foreign and general relations |
| 421 | General works |
| .5 | Relations with individual countries, A-Z |

        For list of countries, see pp. 212-214

|||
|---|---|
| 422 | Biography (General) |

        For collective or individual biography of a specific period, <u>see</u> the period

**Ethnography**

|||
|---|---|
| .5 | General works |
| | **Maoris** |
| | Biography |
| |   Including portraits |
| .8 | Collective |
| .82 | Individual, A-Z |
| 423.A1A-Z | General works |
| .A15 | Study and teaching |

```
                 New Zealand
                   Ethnography
                     Maoris - Continued
   423.A2-Z              Special topics, A-Z

                    .A35   Agriculture
                           Amusements, see .G3
                    .A55   Antiquities
                           Art, see N
                    .A85   Astronomy

                    .B6    Boats.  Canoes
                           Canoes, see .B6
                    .C5    Children.  Youth
                    .C56   Chronology
                    .C8    Criminal justice system

                    .E3    Economic conditions
                           Education, see LC3501.M3
                    .E66   Employment

                    .F5    Fishing
                    .F8    Funeral rites and ceremonies

                    .G3    Games.  Amusements
                           Government, see .P63
                    .G6    Government relations

                    .H8    Hunting
                    .I4    Implements
                    .I53   Industries.  Material culture (General)

                    .J4    Jewelry
                    .K54   Kings and rulers
                    .L35   Land tenure

                           Material culture, see .I53
                    .M38   Medicine
                    .M42   Meetinghouses

                    .P63   Politics and government
                    .P66   Population
```

                    **New Zealand**
                     **Ethnography**
                      **Maoris**
    423.A2-Z              Special topics, A-Z - Continued

                            Religion, see BL2615
                  .R55    Rites and ceremonies

                  .S6     Social conditions
                  .S63    Social life and customs

                  .T26    Tattooing
                  .T4     Textiles

                  .W35    Warfare
                          Youth, see .C5

    424              Individual tribes, A-Z

                  .N37    Ngaa Rauru
                  .N4     Ngaitahu

                  .N44    Ngati Toa

      .5            Other elements in the population, A-Z

                  .C5     Chinese
                  .C76    Croats

                  .E27    East Indians
                  .I8     Italians

                  .P6     Polynesians

                  .S2     Samoans
                  .S3     Scotch

                  .Y84    Yugoslavs

    427              Other

**New Zealand** - Continued
  **Local history and description**
428        Wellington
430        Other cities, regions, etc., A-Z

      e. g.  .A35  Akaroa
              .A4   Alps, Southern
                    Including Arthur's Pass,
                     Mount Cook, etc.
              .A5   Amuri County

             .A79  Auckland (Provincial District)
             .A8   Auckland (City)
             .A83  Auckland Islands

             .B15  Banks Peninsula
             .B2   Bay of Islands

             .C3   Canterbury
             .C48  Chatham Islands
             .C5   Christchurch
             .C6   Cook Islands

             .D8   Dunedin
             .E36  Egmont, Mount

             .G7   Great Barrier Island
             .H33  Hawke's Bay

             .L9   Lyttelton
             .M35  Marlborough

             .N38  Nelson (Provincial District)
             .N4   New Plymouth
             .N5   Niue (Savage Island)

             .O8   Otago

                **New Zealand**
                  **Local history and description**

430                     Other cities, regions, etc., A-Z - Continued

                           e. g.    .P34    Palmerston North

                                      .P8     Pukapuka (Island)

                                      .R6     Rotorua

                                      .S6     Southland

                                      .S7     Stewart Island

                                      .W25    Wakatipu (Lake)
                                      .W3     Wanganui
                                      .W4     Westland

(450-480)              Tasmania (Van Diemen's Land), see DU182+

490                    Melanesia (General)
                          For individual islands or groups of islands, see
                             DU520+
500                    Micronesia (General)
                          For individual islands or groups of islands, see
                             DU520+
510                    Polynesia (General)
                          For individual islands or groups of islands, see
                             DU520+

## SMALLER ISLAND GROUPS

| | |
|---|---|
| 520 | Admiralty Islands |
| | Auckland Islands, <u>see</u> DU430.A83 |
| | Austral Islands, <u>see</u> DU900 |
| | |
| 540 | Banks Islands |
| | **Bismarck Archipelago** |
| | Cf. DU739+, Territory of New Guinea, Northeast New Guinea |
| 550 | General works |
| 553 | Individual islands or groups of islands, A-Z |

Admiralty Islands, <u>see</u> DU520

.L4   Lesu

.N35  New Britain (Neu Pommern, New Pomerania)
.N4   New Ireland (Neu Mecklenburg, New Mecklenburg)

**Caroline Islands**

| | |
|---|---|
| 560 | Periodicals. Societies. Serials |
| 563 | General works. Description and travel |
| | **History** |
| 565 | General works |
| 567 | Modern |
| 568 | Individual islands, groups of islands, cities, etc., A-Z |

.H3   Hall Islands
.I3   Ifalik (Ifaluk)

.K67  Kosrae
.L6   Losap

.M6   Mokil
.N6   Nomoi (Mortlock) Islands

          **Smaller Island Groups**
             **Caroline Islands**

568                 Individual islands, groups of islands, cities, etc., A-Z - Continued

                     Pelew (Palau) Islands, see DU780
           .P7   Ponape (Ascension)
           .P8   Puluwat (Poloat, Polowat)

           .T7   Truk Islands
           .U5   Ulithi (Uluthi)

           .Y3   Yap (Uap)

          Cook Islands, see DU430.C6
          Dangerous Islands, see DU890
580           D'Entrecasteaux Islands
590           Ellice Islands.  Tuvalu
600           Fiji Islands
          Friendly Islands, see DU880
          Gambier Islands, see DU680
615           Gilbert Islands.  Kiribati
          Guam, see DU647

          **Hawaiian Islands.  Hawaii**
620           Periodicals.  Societies.  Serials
          Collected works
   .3            Several authors
   .4             Pamphlet collections
   .5            Individual authors
   .6             Pamphlet collections
621           Directories
   .5       Monumental and picturesque views
622           Gazetteers.  Handbooks.  Guidebooks
          General works.  Description and travel
623           Through 1950
             For early periods to 1800, see DU626+
   .2         1951-1980
   .25        1981-
624           Antiquities
   .5        Social life and customs.  Civilization.  Intellectual life

                    Smaller Island Groups
                      Hawaiian Islands.  Hawaii - Continued
                        Ethnography

| | |
|---|---|
| 624.6 | General works |
| .65 | Polynesian Hawaiians |
| .7 | Other elements in the population, A-Z |

                          .A85  Asians (General)
                          .C5   Chinese

                          .F4   Filipinos
                                Haoles, see .W45

                          .J3   Japanese
                          .K67  Koreans

                          .P67  Portuguese

                          .R87  Russians
                          .R97  Ryukyuans

                          .S36  Samoans

                          .W45  Whites.  Haoles

                    Biography (Collective)
                        For individual biography, see the specific
                          period, reign, or place

| | |
|---|---|
| .9 | General works |
| | Houses, noble families, etc. |
| .95 | General works |
| .96 | Individual houses, families, etc., A-Z |

                          .K35  Kamehameha, House of

Smaller Island Groups
  Hawaiian Island.  Hawaii - Continued
    History
625           General works
  .8          Study and teaching
                Class catalogs of audiovisual materials in
                  .Z9A-Z
            By period
626           To 1778.  Discovery by Captain James Cook
            1778-1900
627           General works
  .1          Kamehameha I, 1784-1819
  .11         Kamehameha II, 1819-1824
  .12         Kamehameha III, 1824-1854
  .13         Kamehameha IV, 1854-1863
  .14         Kamehameha V, 1863-1872
  .15         Lunalilo, 1872-1874
  .16         Kalakaua, 1874-1891
  .17         Biography and memoirs of contemporaries,
                  1784-1891

                .A7  Armstrong, Richard

                .B4  Bishop, Bernice Pauahi

  .18         Liliuokalani, 1891-1893
            Revolution of 1893-1898
  .19           Sources and documents
  .2            General works

```
                    Smaller Island Groups
                      Hawaiian Islands.  Hawaii
                        History
                          By period
                            1778-1900 - Continued
                              Annexation to United States
         627.3                   Sources and documents
           .4                    General works
           .5                Hawaii (Territory), 1900-1959
                               .A1-5  Sources and documents
                               .A6-Z  General works
           .7                Biography and memoirs, 1891-1959

                               .A2A-Z  Collective
                               .A3-Z   Individual, A-Z

                                  .B3    Baldwin, Henry Perrine

                                  .D65   Dole, Sanford Ballard

                                  .F3    Farrington, Wallace Rider

                             State, 1959-
           .8                  General works
                             Biography and memoirs
           .82                  Collective
           .83                  Individual, A-Z

         628           Islands, counties, etc., A-Z

                         .H25   Haleakala National Park
                         .H28   Hawaii (Island).  Hawaii County
                         .H3    Hawaii National Park
                         .H33   Hawaii Volcanoes National Park

                         .K3    Kauai (Kaieiewaho)

                         .L3    Lanai
                         .L4    Laysan
```

Smaller Island Groups
Hawaiian Islands.  Hawaii

628                Islands, counties, etc., A-Z - Continued

  .M3 Maui

  .M5 Midway Islands
  .M7 Molokai

  .N55 Niihau

  .O3 Oahu

629                Cities, volcanoes, etc., A-Z

  .H2 Haleakala

  .H5 Hilo
  .H7 Honolulu

  .K32 Kailua (Hawaii Co.)
  .K5 Kilauea

  .M34 Mauna Loa

  .P3 Parker Ranch

Hervey Islands, see DU430.C6
Kiribati, see DU615
**Northern Mariana Islands.  Ladrone Islands**
640                Periodicals.  Societies.  Serials
643                General works.  Description and travel
645                History
  Individual islands, cities, etc.
647                 Guam
648                 Other, A-Z

   e. g.  .S35  Saipan

**Smaller Island Groups - Continued**

Lagoon Islands, <u>see</u> DU590

| | |
|---|---|
| 650 | Line Islands |
| 660 | Louisiade Archipelago |
| | Low Archipelago, <u>see</u> DU890 |
| 670 | Loyalty Islands |
| 680 | Mangareva Islands |
| | Mariana Islands, <u>see</u> DU640+ |
| | Marquesas Islands |
| 700 | General works |
| 701 | Individual islands, A-Z |

       .F3   Fatuhiva Island

       .H5   Hivaoa Island

       .N8   Nuku-hiva Island

| | |
|---|---|
| 710 | Marshall Islands |
| 715 | Nauru |
| | Navigators' Islands, <u>see</u> DU810+ |
| 720 | New Caledonia |
| | **New Guinea** |
| 739 | General works |
| 740 | Papua New Guinea (Table I)[1] |
| |     Including works on Papua and New Guinea (Territory) |
| | **Irian Jaya.   Irian Barat.   Netherlands New Guinea** |
| 744 | General works.   Description and travel |
| | Ethnography |
| .3 |     General works |
| .35 |     Individual elements in the population, A-Z |

       .A82   Asmat

       .D32   Dani

---

[1]

For subarrangement, <u>see</u> Tables, p. 215

       **Smaller Island Groups**
         **New Guinea**
           **Irian Jaya.   Irian Barat.   Netherlands New Guinea**
            Ethnography

744.35              Individual elements in the population,
                 A-Z - Continued

                .E56   Eipo

                      Huli, <u>see</u> DU740

                .J28   Jalé
                .J32   Jaqai

                .K33   Kaowerawédj
                .K34   Kapauku

                .M33   Mandobo
                .M34   Marind
                .M42   Mejprat

                .N32   Nalum

                .P33   Papuans (General)

                .Y44   Yei

     .5               History
                 Biography
746.A2A-Z          Collective
    .A3-Z          Individual, A-Z

                .M5   Miklukha-Maklaĭ, Nikolaĭ Nikolaevich

                .M8   Murray, Sir Hubert (Sir John Hubert
                      P.)
747             Local, A-Z

                .S8   Sukarno, Mount

**Smaller Island Groups** - Continued

| | |
|---|---|
| 760 | New Hebrides.  Vanuatu |
| | Paumotu Islands, <u>see</u> DU890 |
| 780 | Pelew (Palau) Islands |
| 790 | Phoenix Islands |
| 800 | Pitcairn Island |
| | **Samoan Islands** |
| 810 | Periodicals.  Societies.  Serials |
| 812 | Handbooks |
| 813 | General works.  Description and travel |
| 814 | Antiquities |
| | **History** |
| 815 | General works |
| 816 | Early |
| | Modern.  European colonization |
| 817.A2-5 | Sources and documents |
| .A6-Z | General works |
| .2 | Revolution of 1899 |
| 818 | Biography and memoirs |
| | .A2A-Z  Collective |
| | .A3-Z   Individual, A-Z |
| | .W4  Westbrook, George Egerton L. |
| 819.A1 | American Samoa |
| .A2 | Western Samoa |
| | Formerly German Samoa |
| .A3-Z | Individual islands, cities, etc. |
| | .M3  Manua |
| | .P3  Pagopago |
| | Sandwich Islands, <u>see</u> DU620+ |
| 840 | Santa Cruz Islands |
| 850 | Solomon Islands |
| 860 | Suvarrow (Suvaroff, Suwaroff) Islands |
| 870 | Tahiti and Society Islands |

**Smaller Island Groups** - Continued

Tokelau Islands, <u>see</u> DU910

| | |
|---|---|
| 880 | Tonga Islands |
| 885 | Trobriand Islands |
| 890 | Tuamotu Islands |
| 900 | Tubuai Islands |
| | Tuvalu, <u>see</u> DU590 |
| 910 | Union Islands |
| | Vanuatu, <u>see</u> DU760 |
| 920 | Wallis Archipelago |
| | Wellesley Islands, <u>see</u> DU280.W4 |
| | |
| 950 | Other islands, A-Z |

Auckland Islands, <u>see</u> DU430.A83

.C5    Clipperton Island

Easter Island, <u>see</u> F3169

.W28   Wake Island

| | |
|---|---|
| 101 | Periodicals.  Societies |
| 103 | Congresses |
| 105 | Collections |
| 115 | General works |
| 118 | Popular works |
| 120 | Pamphlets, etc. |
| | Biography and memoirs |

     Including biography of persons identified primarily
      with gypsies
      Cf. TR681.G9, Photographic portraits

| | |
|---|---|
| 125 | Collective |
| 127 | Individual, A-Z |

       e. g.    .P4   Petulengro, Gipsy

**History**

| | |
|---|---|
| (131) | General works, <u>see</u> DX115 |
| 135 | Origin |
| 137 | Ancient |
| 141 | Medieval |
| | Modern |
| 145 | General works |

     By region or country, <u>see</u> DX201+

| | |
|---|---|
| 151 | Beliefs.  Superstition.  Religion |
| | Education, <u>see</u> LC3503+ |
| 155 | Magic.  Fortune-telling, etc. |
| 157 | Folklore |
| | Music, <u>see</u> M1706+; ML248+, ML3593 |
| (161) | Language and literature, <u>see</u> PK2896+ |
| 171 | Trades.  Arts.  Occupations |
| 175 | Wagons.  Caravans |

By region or country

| | |
|---|---|
| 201 | United States |
| 205 | Other American (not A-Z) |
| | Europe |
| | General works, see DX145 |
| 211 | Great Britain |
| 213 | England |
| 215 | Scotland |
| 216 | Wales |
| 217 | Ireland |
| 221 | Austria |
| .5 | Bulgaria |
| 222 | Czechoslovakia |
| 223 | Hungary |
| 224 | Romania |
| 227 | France |
| 229 | Germany |
| 232 | Greece |
| 233 | Italy |
| 235 | Netherlands |
| 237 | Belgium |
| 241 | Soviet Union |
| 242 | Poland |
| 245 | Scandinavian countries |
| 247 | Finland |
| 251 | Spain |
| 255 | Portugal |
| 261 | Switzerland |
| 265 | Turkey and Balkan Peninsula |
| 271 | Yugoslavia |
| | **Asia** |
| 281 | General works |
| 283 | India |
| 289 | Other Asian (not A-Z) |
| | **Africa** |
| 291 | General works |
| 293 | Egypt |
| 299 | Other African (not A-Z) |
| 301 | Other regions or countries (not A-Z) |

Abyssinia, see .E8
Afghanistan ................ .A3
Africa .................... .A35
  Africa, Central ........ .A352
  Africa, East ........... .A353
  Africa, Eastern ........ .A354
  Africa, North .......... .A355
  Africa, Northeast ...... .A3553
  Africa, Northwest ...... .A3554
  Africa, Southern ....... .A356
  Africa, Sub-Saharan .... .A357
  Africa, West ........... .A358
Albania ................... .A38
Algeria ................... .A4
America ................... .A45
Andorra ................... .A48
Angola .................... .A5
Antarctic regions ......... .A6
Antiqua ................... .A63
Arab countries ............ .A65
Argentina ................. .A7
Armenia ................... .A75
Asia ...................... .A78
  Asia, Central .......... .A783
  Asia, East, see .E18
  Asia, Southeastern ..... .A785
  Asia, Southwestern, see .N33
Australia ................. .A8
Austria ................... .A9

Bahamas ................... .B24
Bahrain ................... .B26
Balkan Peninsula .......... .B28
Bangladesh ................ .B3
Barbados .................. .B35
Belgium ................... .B4
Belize .................... .B42
Bengal .................... .B43
Benin ..................... .B45
Bhutan .................... .B47
Bolivia ................... .B5
Botswana .................. .B55
Brazil .................... .B6
British Guiana, see .G95
British Honduras, see .B42
Brunei .................... .B7
Bulgaria .................. .B9
Burkina Faso, see .U65

Burma ..................... .B93
Burundi ................... .B94
Byzantine Empire ........ .B97

Cambodia, see .K3
Cameroon .................. .C17
Canada .................... .C2
Canary Island ............ .C23
Caribbean area ........... .C27
Cayman Islands ........... .C29
Central African Republic. .C33
Central America ......... .C35
Central Europe .......... .C36
Ceylon, see .S72
Chad ...................... .C45
Chile ..................... .C5
China ..................... .C6
Colombia .................. .C7
Communist countries ..... .C725
Congo (Brazzaville) ..... .C74
Costa Rica ............... .C8
Cuba ...................... .C9
Cyprus .................... .C93
Czechoslovakia ........... .C95

Dahomey, see .B45
Denmark ................... .D4
Developing countries .... .D44
Djibouti .................. .D5
Dominican Republic ...... .D65
Dutch East Indies, see .I5

East ...................... .E16
East Asia ................. .E18
Ecuador ................... .E2
Egypt ..................... .E3
El Salvador, see .S2
Ethiopia .................. .E8
Europe .................... .E85
  Europe, Central, see .C36
  Europe, Eastern ....... .E852
  Europe, Northern ...... .E853
  Europe, Southern ...... .E854
  Europe, Western, see .E85
European Economic Community
  countries ............. .E86

Falkland Islands ......... .F3
Fiji .................... .F4
Finland ................. .F5
France .................. .F8
French Guiana ........... .F9

Gabon ................... .G2
Gambia .................. .G25
Germany ................. .G3
Germany (East) .......... .G35
Germany (West), see .G3
Ghana ................... .G4
Great Britain ........... .G7
Greece .................. .G8
Greenland ............... .G83
Grenada ................. .G84
Guam .................... .G85
Guatemala ............... .G9
Guinea .................. .G92
Guinea-Bissau ........... .G93
Guyana .................. .G95

Haiti ................... .H2
Holland, see .N4
Honduras ................ .H8
Hong Kong ............... .H85
Hungary ................. .H9

Iceland ................. .I2
India ................... .I4
Indochina ............... .I48
Indonesia ............... .I5
Iran .................... .I7
Iraq .................... .I72
Ireland ................. .I73
Islamic countries ....... .I74
Islamic Empire .......... .I742
Israel .................. .I75
Italy ................... .I8
Ivory Coast ............. .I9

Jamaica ................. .J25
Japan ................... .J3

Kampuchea ............... .K3
Kenya ................... .K4
Kiribati ................ .K5

Korea ................... .K6
Korea (North) ........... .K7
Korea (South), see .K6
Kuwait .................. .K9

Laos .................... .L28
Latin America ........... .L29
Lebanon ................. .L4
Lesotho ................. .L5
Liberia ................. .L7
Libya ................... .L75
Liechtenstein ........... .L76
Luxembourg .............. .L9

Macao ................... .M25
Macedonia ............... .M27
Madagascar .............. .M28
Malagasy, see .M28
Malawi .................. .M3
Malay Archipelago ....... .M35
Malaya, see .M4
Malaysia ................ .M4
Maldives ................ .M415
Mali .................... .M42
Malta ................... .M43
Mauritania .............. .M44
Mauritius ............... .M45
Melanesia ............... .M5
Mexico .................. .M6
Micronesia .............. .M625
Monaco .................. .M63
Mongolia ................ .M65
Montserrat .............. .M7
Morocco ................. .M8
Mozambique .............. .M85

Namibia ................. .N3
Near East ............... .N33
Nepal ................... .N35
Netherlands ............. .N4
New Guinea .............. .N43
New Zealand ............. .N45
Nicaragua ............... .N5
Niger ................... .N55
Nigeria ................. .N6
North America ........... .N7
Northern Rhodesia, see .Z33
Norway .................. .N8
Nyasaland, see .M3

| | |
|---|---|
| Oceania | .O3 |
| Oman | .O5 |
| | |
| Pacific area | .P16 |
| Pakistan | .P18 |
| Palestine | .P19 |
| Panama | .P2 |
| Papua New Guinea | .P26 |
| Paraguay | .P3 |
| Peru | .P4 |
| Philippines | .P6 |
| Poland | .P7 |
| Polynesia | .P75 |
| Portugal | .P8 |
| Puerto Rico | .P9 |
| | |
| Qatar | .Q2 |
| | |
| Réunion | .R4 |
| Rhodesia, Northern, see .Z33 | |
| Rhodesia, Southern, see .Z55 | |
| Romania | .R6 |
| Russia, see .S65 | |
| Rwanda | .R95 |
| | |
| Sahel | .S15 |
| Saint Kitts-Nevis-Anguilla | .S17 |
| Salvador | .S2 |
| San Marino | .S27 |
| Saudi Arabia | .S33 |
| Scandinavia | .S34 |
| Senegal | .S38 |
| Seychelles | .S45 |
| Sierra Leone | .S5 |
| Singapore | .S55 |
| Somalia | .S58 |
| South Africa | .S6 |
| South America | .S63 |
| South Asia | .S64 |
| Soviet Union | .S65 |

| | |
|---|---|
| Spain | .S7 |
| Sri Lanka | .S72 |
| Sudan | .S73 |
| Surinam | .S75 |
| Swaziland | .S78 |
| Sweden | .S8 |
| Switzerland | .S9 |
| Syria | .S95 |
| | |
| Taiwan | .T28 |
| Tanganyika, see .T34 | |
| Tanzania | .T34 |
| Thailand | .T5 |
| Tibet | .T55 |
| Togo | .T6 |
| Trinidad and Tobago | .T7 |
| Tunisia | .T8 |
| Turkey | .T9 |
| | |
| Uganda | .U33 |
| United Arab Emirates | .U5 |
| United States | .U6 |
| Upper Volta | .U65 |
| Uruguay | .U8 |
| | |
| Vatican City | .V3 |
| Venezuela | .V4 |
| Vietnam | .V5 |
| | |
| Yemen | .Y4 |
| Yemen (People's Democratic Republic) | .Y45 |
| Yugoslavia | .Y8 |
| | |
| Zaire | .Z28 |
| Zambia | .Z33 |
| Zimbabwe | .Z55 |

## COUNTRIES AND REGIONS WITH SINGLE NUMBER OR CUTTER NUMBER

| I | II | III | |
|---|---|---|---|
| .A2A-Z | .xA2A-Z | .xA2-29 | Periodicals. Societies. Serials |
| .A3A-Z | .xA3A-Z | .xA3-39 | Sources and documents |
| .A5-Z | .xA5-Z | .xA5-Z | General works |
| .2 | .x2 | .x2 | Description and travel. Guidebooks. Gazetteers |
| .3 | .x3 | .x3 | Antiquities |
| .4 | .x4 | .x4 | Social life and customs. Civilization. Intellectual life |
| .42 | .x42 | .x42 | Ethnography |
| | | | **History** |
| .5 | .x5 | .x5 | General works |
| .6 | .x6 | .x6 | Biography (Collective) |
| | | | Political history. Foreign and general relations |
| .62 | .x62 | .x62 | General works |
| | | | By period, <u>see</u> the specific period |
| .63 | .x63 | .x63 | Relations with individual countries, A-Z |
| | | | For list of countries, <u>see</u> pp. 188-190 |
| | | | **By period** |
| | | | Early |
| .65 | .x65 | .x65 | General works |
| .66 | .x66 | .x66 | Biography and memoirs |
| | | | .A2A-Z  Collective |
| | | | .A3-Z  Individual, A-Z |
| | | | Colonial |
| .7 | .x7 | .x7 | General works |
| .72 | .x72 | .x72 | Biography and memoirs |
| | | | .A2A-Z  Collective |
| | | | .A3-Z  Individual, A-Z |
| | | | 20th century |
| .75 | .x75 | .x75 | General works |
| .76 | .x76 | .x76 | Biography and memoirs |
| | | | .A2A-Z  Collective |
| | | | .A3-Z  Individual, A-Z |
| | | | Independent |
| .8 | .x8 | .x8 | General works |
| .82 | .x82 | .x82 | Biography and memoirs |
| | | | .A2A-Z  Collective |
| | | | .A3-Z  Individual, A-Z |
| .9 | .x9 | .x9 | Local, A-Z |

## CITIES WITH SINGLE NUMBER OR CUTTER NUMBER

To be used only where indicated in schedules

| IV | V[1] | |
|---|---|---|
| .A2A-Z | .x | Periodicals. Societies. Serials |
| .A3A-Z | .x2 | Museums, exhibitions, etc. |
| | | Subarranged by author |
| .A4A-Z | .x3 | Guidebooks. Gazetteers. Directories |
| .A5-Z | .x4 | General works. Description |
| .1 | .x43 | Views |
| .13 | .x45 | Addresses, essays, lectures. Anecdotes, etc. |
| .15 | .x47 | Antiquities |
| .2 | .x5 | Social life and customs. Civilization. Intellectual life |
| | | History |
| .23 | .x53 | Biography[2] |
| .25 | .x55 | Historiography. Study and teaching |
| .3 | .x57 | General works |
| .4 | .x6 | Sections, districts, suburbs, etc.[2] |
| .5 | .x65 | Monuments, statues, etc.[2] |
| .6 | .x7 | Parks, squares, cemeteries, etc.[2] |
| .7 | .x75 | Streets, bridges, etc.[2] |
| .8 | .x8 | Buildings[2] |
| .9 | .x9 | Elements in the population[2] |
| .95 | .x95 | Natural features such as mountains, rivers, etc., A-Z |

---

[1] The x in Table V is the Cutter number for the city

[2] Subdivided as follows:
  Table IV
    .A2A-Z  Collective
    .A3-Z   Individual, A-Z

  Table V
    .A2A-Z  Collective
    .A3-Z   Individual, A-Z

## INDIVIDUAL BIOGRAPHY

Use the tables below to subarrange numbers and Cutters for individual persons under each class of the D schedule providing for biography and memoirs, e. g. DA556.9.C55, Churchill, Winston Leonard Spencer, Sir.

> Exception:  For class numbers designating individual reigns, including the life of a rulers, e. g. DA539, General works on life and reign of William IV, Cutter only for the author of the works without further subarrangement.

| VI<br>One no. | VII<br>Cutter no. | |
|---|---|---|
|  | .x | Cutter for the individual |
| .A2 | .xA2 | Collected works.  By date[1] |
| .A25 | .xA25 | Selected works.  Selections.  By date[1]<br>    Including quotations |
| .A3 | .xA3 | Autobiography, diaries, etc.  By date |
| .A4 | .xA4 | Letters.  By date |
| .A5 | .xA5 | Speeches, essays, and lectures.  By date<br>    Including interviews |
| .A6-Z | .xA6-Z | Biography and criticism<br>    Including criticism of selected works,<br>        quotations, autobiography, letters,<br>        speeches, etc. |

---

[1]
Class here collected or selected works by an individual on general historical or political topics pertaining to the period during which the individual lived.  For the collected or selected works of an individual on a special topic, see the topic.

## A

Abbas, Khedive of Egypt
  I: DT104.7
  II: DT107.6
Abbas Hilmi, Khedive of Egypt:
  DT107.6
'Abd-al-Ḳādir ibn Muḥyi al-Dīn,
  Amir of Mascara: DT294.7.A3
Abd el-Krim: DT324.92.A3
Abdurahman, A.: DT1927.A34
Abolition of slavery, 1834
  (South Africa): DT1845
Abron (African people)
  in
    Ivory Coast: DT545.45.A27
Abū Jirāb (Egypt): DT73.A13
Abū Ṣīr Site (Egypt): DT73.A14
Abu Sunbul (Egypt): DT73.A15
Abydos (Egypt): DT73.A16
Abyssinia: DT371+
Acoli (African people):
  DT155.2.A35
Adamawa (Emirate): DT532.115
Addis Ababa (Ethiopia): DT390.A3
Adelaide (Australia): DU328
Administration of the French East
  India Company (Mauritius):
  DT469.M465+
Admiralty Islands: DU520
Afghans
  in
    Australia: DU122.P87
Africa: DT1+
African Lakes Company (Malawi):
  DT3211+
Afrikaaner Republic of Upingtonia,
  1885-1887: DT1610
Afrikaaner Trek, 1878-1879: DT1601
Afrikaner centennial, 1936-1938
  (Union of South Africa): DT1937.5
Afrikaner domination (Union of
  South Africa): DT1938+
Afrikaner Rebellion, 1914 (Union
  of South Africa): DT1933
Afrikaners
  in
    Namibia: DT1558.A46
    South Africa: DT1768.A57
Afro-Americans
  in
    Ghana: DT510.43.A37
Agalega Island: DT469.M491

Agni (African people)
  in
    Ivory Coast: DT545.45.A58
Agostinho Neto: DT1426
Agriculture, Maori:
  DU423.A35
Ahansala (African people)
  in
    Morocco: DT313.3.A35
Ahidjo administration (Cameroon):
  DT576+
Ahmad Seif-ed Din, Prince of
  Egypt: DT107.2.A5
Ait Atta (Berber people)
  in
    Morocco: DT313.3.A37
Aja (African people)
  in
    Benin: DT541.45.A33
    Togo: DT582.45.A34
Ajjer
  in
    Algeria: DT283.6.A44
Aka (African people)
  in
    Central African Republic:
      DT546.345.A35
Akans (African people)
  in
    Ghana: DT510.43.A53
Akaroa (New Zealand): DU430.A35
Akāshah Site (Sudan): DT159.9.A35
Akhmīm (Egypt): DT73.A28
Aksha (Sudan): DT159.9.A37
Aksum Kingdom (Ethiopia):
  DT390.A88
Al-Mina (Egypt): DT73.A3
Aldeia da Madragoa (Mozambique):
  DT3415.C55
Alexandria (Egypt)
  Ancient: DT73.A4
  Modern: DT154.A4
Algeria: DT271+
Algerian Revolution, 1954-1962:
  DT295+
Algerians
  in
    Tunisia: DT253.2.A43
Algiers (Algeria): DT299.A5
Ali Bey: DT98.5
Alps, Southern (New Zealand):
  DU430.A4
Altars (Egyptology): DT68.8

Althiburos (Tunisia):
DT269.A48
Alur (African people)
in
Zaire: DT650.A48
Alves, Nito: DT1424.A58
Alyawara (Australian people):
DU125.A49
Amaa (African people)
in
Sudan: DT155.2.A53
Ambato-Boeni (Madagascar):
DT469.M37A52
Ambo (African people)
in
Zambia: DT3058.A63
Ambrizete (Angola): DT1465.N94
Amenhetep IV, King of Egypt:
DT87.4+
American Colonization Society
settlements (Liberia): DT633+
American Samoa: DU819.A1
Americans
in
Australia: DU122.A5
Amharas (African people)
in
Ethiopia: DT380.4.A43
Amin regime: DT433.283
Amirante Islands: DT469.A6
Amulets (Egyptology): DT62.A5
Amuri County (New Zealand):
DU430.A5
Amusements, Maori: DU423.G3
Ancient Egypt: DT57+
Andrade, Mario Pinto de:
DT1417.A54
Androy (Madagascar): DT469.M37A53
Angas (African people)
in
Nigeria: DT515.45.A53
Angas, George Fife: DU322.A5
Anglo-Egyptian Sudan: DT154.1+
Anglo-German accords to Zanzibar
(Kenya): DT433.57+
Angoche (Mozambique): DT3415.A65
Angola: DT1251+
Angola Afrikaaners' resettlement,
1925: DT1634
Annobon Island (Equatorial Guinea):
DT620.9.A65
Antananarivo (Madagascar):
DT469.M38T34

Antandroy (Malagasy people):
DT469.M777A58
Anti-Asian riots, 1897 (Natal):
DT2263
Antinoopolis (Egypt): DT73.A7
Antiquities, Maori: DU423.A55
António Enes (Mozambique):
DT3415.A65
Antonio Fernandez, Expedition of:
DT2943
Anuaks
in
Sudan: DT155.2.A68
Anyi (African people)
in
Ivory Coast: DT545.45.A58
Apartheid
Namibia: DT1556
South Africa: DT1757
Aphroditopolis (Egypt): DT73.A75
Arab and Berber Almoravid
domination (Mauritania):
DT554.65+
Arab and Swahili Expeditions
(Zambia): DT3085
Arab conquest (North Africa):
DT173
Arab domination (Mozambique):
DT3345+
Arab penetration (Kenya):
DT433.565+
Arabi Pasha: DT107.4
Arabs
in
Algeria: DT283.4+
Morocco: DT313.4+
Sudan: DT155.2.A78
Arameans
in
Egypt: DT72.A73
Armant (Egypt): DT73.A8
Armed struggle for national
liberation, 1966-    (Namibia):
DT1645
Armenians
in
Australia: DU122.A7
Egypt: DT72.A75
Ethiopia: DT380.4.A7
Arminnã West Site (Egypt):
DT73.A812
Armstrong, Richard: DU627.17.A7
Arnhem Land (Australia):
DU398.A7

Balla Balla (Zimbabwe): DT3025.M43
Ballarat (Australia): DU230.B3
Balts
    in
        Australia: DU122.B34
Baluba (African people)
    in
        Zaire: DT650.L8
Bambara (African people)
    in
        Mali: DT551.45.B35
Bambata Rebellion, 1907 (Natal):
    DT2267
Bambute (African people)
    in
        Zaire: DT650.B36
Bamileke (African people)
    in
        Cameroon: DT571.B34
Bamun (African people)
    in
        Cameroon: DT571.B35
Bana (African people)
    in
        Cameroon: DT571.B36
Banda, Hastings Kamuzu, 1964-    :
    DT3236
Bangweulu Lake and Swamp (Zambia):
    DT3140.B36
Bani Hassan (Egypt): DT73.B4
Banjal (African people)
    in
        Senegal: DT549.45.B35
Banks Islands: DU540
Banks Peninsula (New Zealand):
    DU430.B15
Bantus: DT16.B2
Baoule (African people)
    in
        Ivory Coast: DT545.45.B36
Bara (Malagasy people):
    DT469.M277B37
Barabaig (African people)
    in
        Tanzania: DT443.3.B37
Barbary States: DT181+
Bariba (African people)
    in
        Benin: DT541.45.B37
Barmera (Australia): DU330.B3
Barotseland (Zambia): DT3140.W48
Barqah (Libya): DT238.C8
Barreto, Francisco: DT3353.B38

Barreto expedition, 1572
    (Mozambique): DT3355
Barwe (African people)
    in
        Mozambique: DT3328.B37
        Zimbabwe: DT2913.B38
Bas-Congo: DT665.B3
Basa (African people)
    in
        Cameroon: DT571.B37
Basakata (African people)
    in
        Zaire: DT650.B365
Bashi (African people)
    in
        Zaire: DT650.B366
Basku (African people)
    in
        Zaire: DT650.B37
Bassari (African people)
    in
        Senegal: DT549.45.B37
Bassonge (African people)
    in
        Zaire: DT650.S55
Basuto War (South Africa)
    I: DT1865
    II: DT1869
    III: DT1873
Basutoland: DT2541+
Batheon
    I: DT2493.B37
    II: DT2493.B38
Baths (Egyptology): DT62.B3
Batlokwa uprising under
    Mantatisi, 1922: DT2338
Battle at Sekhukhune's Stronghold,
    1879: DT2784
Battle of Lubuya, 1854: DT2782
Bavëk (African people)
    in
        Cameroon: DT571.B38
Bavili (African people)
    in
        Zaire: DT650.B375
Bavuma (African people)
    in
        Uganda: DT433.245.B38
Bay of Islands (New Zealand):
    DU430.B2
Bayaka (African people)
    in
        Zaire: DT650.B38

Chariots (Egyptology): DT62.C48
Chatham Islands (New Zealand):
  DU430.C48
Chegutu (Zimbabwe): DT3025.C54
Cherchel (Algeria): DT299.C5
Chewa
  in
      Malawi: DT3192.C54
Chibia (Angola): DT1465.C55
Chicualacuala (Mozambique):
  DT3415.C54
Chikerema, James: DT2979.C55
Children, Maori: DU423.C5
Chilembene (Mozambique):
  DT3415.C55
Chilembwe, John: DT3219.C55
Chilembwe Rebellion, 1915
  (Malawi): DT3225
Chilialombwe (Zambia): DT3145.C55
Chimoio (Mozambique): DT3415.C56
Chimurenga (Zimbabwe)
  I:  DT2968
  II: DT2988+
Chinese
  in
      Africa: DT16.C48
      Australia: DU122.C5
      Hawaii: DU624.7.C5
      islands of the East African
        coast: DT468.45.C45
      New Zealand: DU424.5.C5
      Réunion: DT469.R39C48
      South Africa: DT1768.C55
Chinese laborers, Importation of
  (South Africa): DT1922
Chingola (Zambia): DT3145.C56
Chinhoyi (Zimbabwe): DT3025.C55
Chipembere, Masauko: DT3235.C55
Chipembere Rebellion, 1965:
  DT3237
Chipenda, Daniel: DT1417.C55
Chipinga (Zimbabwe): DT3025.C55
Chissano, Joaquim: DT3398
Chivhu (Zimbabwe): DT3025.C56
Chokwe
  in
      Angola: DT1308.C67
      Zambia: DT3058.C56
Chokwe (Mozambique): DT3415.C58
Chopi
  in
      Mozambique: DT3328.C67
Christchurch (New Zealand):
  DU430.C5

Christian, Jacobus: DT1628.C57
Christian, Johannes: DT1608.C57
Christian period (Egyptian
  antiquities): DT69
Chronology, Maori: DU423.C56
Circassians
  in
      Egypt: DT72.C53
Ciskei (South Africa): DT2400.C58
Civil war
  Angola, 1975-    : DT1428
  Eritrea, 1962-    : DT397
  Nigeria, 1967-1970: DT515.836
  Rwanda, 1959-1962: DT450.43
  Sudan, 1956-1972: DT157.67
  Zaire, 1960-1965: DT658.22
Cleopatra, Queen of Egypt:
  DT92.7
Clipperton Island: DU950.C5
Clysma (Egypt): DT73.C55
Cocotiers (Equatorial Guinea):
  DT620.9.E46
Coffins (Egyptology): DT62.C64
Coghlan, Charles, DT2975.C65
Colenso, Battle of, 1899:
  DT1908.C65
Colonies and possessions
  Africa: DT31+
  Oceania: DU28.35+
Colony and Protectorate of
  Nigeria: DT515.75+
Colored people
  in
      South Africa: DT1768.C65
      Zimbabwe: DT2913.C75
Comoro Islands: DT469.C7
Compagnie des Indes Orientales
  (Réunion): DT469.R44+
Conga (Equatorial Guinea):
  DT620.9.E46
Congo (Brazzaville): DT546.2+
Congo (Democratic Republic):
  DT641+
Congo Free State: DT655+
Congo Kingdom: DT654+
Congo River region: DT639
Constantine (Algeria)
  City: DT299.C6
  Department: DT298.C7
Convention of Pretoria, 1881:
  DT2786
Cook, James: DU626
Cook Islands (New Zealand):
  DU430.C6

Futa-Jallon: DT532.13

**G**

G/wi (African people)
  in
    Botswana: DT2458.G27
Ga (African people)
  in
    Ghana: DT510.43.G3
Gaanda (African people)
  in
    Nigeria: DT515.45.G32
Gabbra (African people)
  in
    Kenya: DT433.545.G32
Gabon: DT546.1+
Gaboon: DT546.1+
Gabun: DT546.1+
Gade (African people): DT545.45.G33
Gadjerong (Australian people):
  DU125.G33
Gagou (African people)
  in
    Ivory Coast: DT545.45.G34
Gaika, Xhosa chief: DT1831.G35
Gallas (Galla)
  Ethiopia; DT390.G2
Galwa (African people)
  in
    Gabon: DT546.145.G34
Gambia: DT509+
Gambier Islands: DU680
Games, Maori: DU423.G3
Gaston, Albert: DU372.G3
Gatooma (Zimbabwe): DT3025.K34
Gaza (Mozambique): DT3410.G39
Gazankulu (South Africa):
  DT2400.G39
Gbaya (African people)
  in
    West Africa: DT474.6.G32
Geelong (Australia): DU230.G4
Genya (African people)
  in
    Zaire: DT650.G46
Gere (African people)
  in
    Ivory Coast: DT545.45.G47
Gerf Hussein Temple (Egypt):
  DT73.G47
German claims to the Witu
  Protectorate (Kenya): DT433.57+

German colonization, 1856 (South
  Africa): DT1861
German colony (Togo): DT582.7
German domination
  of
    Burundi: DT450.77+
    Rwanda: DT450.37+
German East Africa: DT436+
German reunification movement,
  1932-1939 (Namibia): DT1636
German settlements (Namibia):
  DT1587+
German South-West Africa:
  DT1603+
Germans
  in
    Australia: DU122.G4
    Egypt: DT72.G4
    Namibia: DT1558.G46
    South Africa: DT1768.G48
Ghana: DT509.97+
Ghana empire: DT532.15
al-Gharbīyah (Egypt): DT137.G5
Ghoya
  in
    South Africa: DT1768.G56
Gilbert Islands: DU615
Gimiras (African people)
  in
    Ethiopia: DT380.4.G35
Giryama (African people)
  in
    Kenya: DT433.545.G55
Gitarama coup d'état, 1961
  (Rwanda): DT450.432
Giuba (Italian Somaliland):
  DT409.G58
Gizeh (Egypt): DT73.G5
Gladstone (Australia): DU280.G5
Goans (African people)
  in
    Mozambique: DT3328.G73
Gold Coast: DT509.97
Gold discovery, 1851 (Australia):
  DU103
Goletta, Siege of: DT262
Gonga (African people)
  in
    Ethiopia: DT380.4.G66
Gonja (African people)
  in
    Ghana: DT510.43.G65
Gordon (Sudan): DT156.6
Gore-Browne, Steward: DT3106.G78

Gourma Kingdoms (Burkina Faso):
  DT555.65+
Gouveia, Manuel Antonio de Sousa:
  DT3364.G68
Gova (African people)
  in
    Zambia: DT3058.G79
    Zimbabwe: DT2913.G68
Government, Maori: DU423.P63
Government relations, Maori:
  DU423.G6
Gowon administration (Nigeria):
  DT515.834+
Graaf-Reinet and Swellendam
  Rebellion, 1795: DT1835
Grain Coast (Liberia): DT633+
Grand Bassa County (Liberia):
  DT637.G7
Great Barrier Island (New Zealand):
  DU430.G7
Great Karoo (South Africa):
  DT2400.G84
Great Trek, 1836-1840 (South
  Africa): DT1853
Great Zimbabwe: DT3025.G84
Greater Khartum (Sudan): DT159.7
Greeks
  in
    Australia: DU122.G7
    Egypt: DT72.G7
    Ethiopia: DT380.4.G72
    Sudan: DT155.2.G74
Griffith, Chief Nathaniel:
  DT2642.G75
Griqua lands, 1861, Purchase of
  (Orange Free State): DT2131
Griqua settlements, 1803 (Orange
  Free State): DT2116
Griqualand, Annexation of:
  DT1886
Griquas
  in
    South Africa: DT1768.G74
Guam: DU647
Guija (Mozambique): DT3415.G85
Guinea: DT543+
Guinea-Bissau: DT613+
Gumeracha (Australia): DU330.G8
Gun War, 1880-1881 (Basutoland):
  DT2648
Gungunhana: DT3364.G86
Gurages (African people)
  in
    Ethiopia: DT380.4.G85

Gurma (African people)
  in
    Benin: DT541.45.G87
    Burkina Faso: DT555.45.G85
Guro (African people)
  in
    Ivory Coast: DT545.45.G87
Gurob (Egypt): DT73.G85
Gurundji (Australian people):
  DU125.G8
Gurunsi (African people)
  in
    Burkina Faso: DT555.45.G87
Guruwe (Zimbabwe): DT3025.G87
Gusii (African people)
  in
    Kenya: DT433.545.G86
Gwari (African people)
  in
    Nigeria: DT515.45.G83
Gwelo (Zimbabwe): DT3025.G89
Gwembe Tonga Uprising, 1909
  (Zambia): DT3097
Gweru (Zimbabwe): DT3025.G89
Gypsies: DX101+


H

Hadiya (African people)
  in
    Ethiopia: DT380.4.H33
Haile Selassie I, Emperor of
  Ethiopia: DT387.7+
Haleakala (Volcano)
  Hawaii: DU629.H2
Haleakala National Park
  (Hawaii): DU628.H25
Hall Islands: DU568.H3
Hamar
  in
    Ethiopia: DT380.4.H36
Hambukushu (African people)
  in
    Botswana: DT2458.H36
Hammamet (Tunisia): DT269.H3
Hanya (African people)
  in
    Angola: DT1308.H35
Haoles
  in
    Hawaii: DU624.7.W45
Haram Zāwiyat al 'Urbān
  (Egypt): DT73.H25

Harar (Ethiopia): DT390.H3
Harare (Zimbabwe): DT3022
Harris, Charles M.: DU372.H34
Hartley (Zimbabwe): DT3025.C54
Hassan II, King of Morocco:
  DT325.92.H37
Hatshepsut, Queen of Egypt:
  DT87.15
Hausas (African people)
  in
    Niger: DT547.45.H38
    Nigeria: DT515.45.H38
    Sudan: DT155.2.H38
Havu (African people)
  in
    Zaire: DT650.H38
Hawaii: DU620+
Hawaii (Island): DU628.H28
Hawaii (Territory), 1900-1959:
  DU627.5+
Hawaii County: DU628.H28
Hawaii National Park: DU628.H3
Hawaii Volcanoes National Park:
  DU628.H33
Hawaiian Islands: DU620+
Hawawish Site (Egypt): DT73.H34
Hawke's Bay (New Zealand):
  DU430.H33
Haya (African people)
  in
    Uganda: DT433.245.H38
Heikum (African people)
  in
    Namibia: DT1558.H45
Heliopolis (Egypt): DT73.H42
Helwan (Egypt): DT154.H5
Henrique de Carvalho (Angola):
  DT1465.S38
Heracleopolis Magna (Egypt):
  DT73.H44
Herero
  in
    Angola: DT1308.H48
    Namibia: DT1558.H47
Herero Uprising, 1896: DT1614
Herero War, 1904-1907: DT1618
Hereroland (Namibia): DT1670.H47
Hermopolis Magna (Egypt): DT73.A85
Hermopolite Nome (Egypt): DT73.H45
Hervey Islands: DU430.C6
Herzog, J.B.M.: DT1927.H47
Hhohho (Swaziland): DT2820.H56
Hierakonpolis (Egypt): DT73.K453
Hilo (Hawaii): DU629.H5

Hima (African people)
  in
    Zaire: DT650.H54
Himba (African people)
  in
    Angola: DT1308.H56
    Namibia: DT1558.H56
Hisn, Kawn al- (Egypt): DT73.H57
Hivaoa Island: DU701.H5
Homelands
  Namibia: DT1557
  South Africa: DT1760
Honolulu (Hawaii): DU629.H7
Horombo (African people)
  in
    Tanzania: DT443.3.H67
Hottentots (African people)
  in
    South Africa: DT1768.K56
Houses (Sudan): DT155.44+
Hova rule (Madagascar):
  DT469.M32+
Hovas
  in
    Madagascar: DT469.M277H68
Huambo (Angola)
  City: DT1465.H83
  Province: DT1450.H83
Huggins, Godfrey: DT2975.H85
Huguenot settlement, 1688:
  DT1823
Huguenots
  in
    South Africa: DT1768.F73
Huila (Angola): DT1450.H85
Huli: DU740
Hungarians
  in
    Australia: DU122.H8
Hunting, Maori: DU423.H8
Hussein Kamil, Sultan of Egypt:
  DT107.7
Hwange (Zimbabwe): DT3025.H93
Hyksos: DT86


I


Ibibios (African people)
  in
    Kenya: DT433.545.I24
    Nigeria: DT515.45.I24
Ibis Nome (Egypt): DT73.I25
Ibrahim, Pasha of Egypt: DT104.5

Karanga Empire: DT1111
Karanis (Egypt): DT73.K33
Karasburg (Namibia): DT1685.K37
Kariba, Lake (Zimbabwe):
  DT3020.K38
Karmah (Sudan): DT159.9.K37
Karnak (Egypt): DT73.K4
Kasai (Zaire): DT665.K28
Kasanga (African people): DT650.K36
Kasena (African people)
  in
    Ghana: DT510.43.K37
Kasongo (Zaire): DT665.M35
Kassinga (Angola): DT1465.K38
Kat River Rebellion, 1851 (South
  Africa): DT1859
Katanga (Zaire): DT665.K3
Kauai (Hawaii): DU628.K3
Kaunda, Kenneth: DT3119
Kaurna (Australian people):
  DU125.K3
Kavango (Namibia): DT1670.K38
Kawa (Egypt): DT73.K45
al Kawn al Ahmar (Egypt):
  DT73.K453
Kazembe III Lukwesa: DT3081.K38
Kazembe IV Keleka: DT3081.K39
Keate, R.W.: DT2254.K43
Keita, Modibo: DT551.82.K44
Kellia Site (Egypt): DT73.K47
Kelly, Edward: DU222.K4
Kemants (African people)
  in
    Ethiopia: DT380.4.K45
Kennedy, Alexander: DU272.K34
Kenya: DT433.5+
Kenya Colony and Protectorate:
  DT433.575+
Kerebe (African people)
  in
    Tanzania: DT443.3.K47
Kereko administration (Benin):
  DT541.845
Kerkouane (Tunisia): DT269.K37
Kgatla (African people)
  in
    Botswana:DT2458.K53
    South Africa: DT1768.K53
    Zimbabwe: DT2913.K53
Khama, Seretse, 1966-1980:
  DT2500
Khama, Tshekedi: DT2493.K53
Khama III, Ngwato chief:
  DT2493.K54

Kharga Oasis (Egypt)
  Ancient: DT73.K5
  Modern: DT154.K6
Khartum (Sudan): DT159.7
Khoikhoi
  in
    South Africa: DT1768.K56
    Southern Africa: DT1058.K56
Khoikhoi War
  I: DT1819
  II: DT1821
Khumir (Tunisia): DT269.K4
Kikuyu (African people):
  DT433.545.K55
Kilauea (Hawaii): DU629.K5
Kilimanjaro (Tanzania):
  DT449.K4
Kilindi (African people)
  in
    Tanzania: DT443.3.K54
Kilwa Kisiwani Island (Tanzania):
  DT449.K45
Kimberley (Australia): DU380.K5
Kimberley (South Africa):
  DT2405.K56
Kimberley, Siege of, 1899-1900
  (South Africa): DT1908.K56
Kings and rulers
  Maori: DU423.K54
  Sudan: DT155.42
Kinshasa (Zaire); DT665.L4
Kipsigis (African people)
  in
    Kenya: DT433.545.K57
Kiribati: DU615
Kirwan, Sir John: DU372.K5
Kisangani (Zaire): DT665.K55
Kitchener (Sudan): DT156.6
Kitwe (Zambia): DT3145.K58
Kivu (Zaire): DT665.K58
Kok, Adam III: DT2127.K65
Kolwezi Massacre, 1978: DT658.25
Kongo (African people)
  in
    Angola: DT1308.K66
Kongo (Angola): DT1465.M42
Kongo River Region: DT639
Koniagui (African people)
  in
    French West Africa:
      DT530.5.K64
Konsos (African people)
  in
    Ethiopia: DT380.4.K65

Malibamatso River (Lesotho):
  DT2680.M35
Malkata Site (Egypt): DT73.M24
Maloti Mountains (Lesotho):
  DT2680.M36
Maltese
  in
      Algeria: DT283.6.M35
      Australia: DU122.M34
Malvernia (Mozambique):
  DT3415.C54
Mamabolo (African people)
  in
      South Africa: DT1768.M36
Mambila (African people)
  in
      Nigeria: DT515.45.M35
Mambwe (African people)
  in
      Zambia: DT3058.M35
Mamprusi (African people)
  in
      Ghana: DT510.43.M35
Mandari (African people):
  DT155.2.M36
Mandela, Nelson: DT1949.M35
Mandela, Winnie: DT1949.M36
Mandingo (African people)
  in
      Gambia: DT509.45.M34
      Guinea: DT543.45.M34
      Guinea-Bissau: DT613.45.M36
      Mali: DT551.45.M36
      West Africa: DT474.6.M36
Mandjildjara (Australian people):
  DU125.M29
Mandobo (African people)
  in
      Irian Jaya: DU744.35.M33
Manetho: DT83.A2
Manganja
  in
      Malawi: DT3192.M35
Mangareva Islands: DU680
Manica (Mozambique): DT3410.M36
Manicaland (Zimbabwe):
  DT3020.M35
Maniema (Zaire): DT665.M35
Manjacaze (Mozambique):
  DT3410.M37
Mantatee: DT2335.M36
Mantatisi: DT2335.M36
Manua: DU819.M3
Manzini (Swaziland): DT2825.M35

Maoris: DU422.8+
Maputo (Mozambique)
  City: DT3412
  Province: DT3410.M38
Marakwet (African people)
  in
      Kenya: DT433.545.M32
Marea (Egypt): DT73.M245
Mariana Islands: DU640+
Marind
  in
      Irian Jaya: DU744.35.M34
Marlborough (New Zealand):
  DU430.M35
Marquesas Islands: DU700+
Marrakesh (Morocco): DT329.M3
Marshall Islands: DU710
Masa (African people)
  in
      Chad: DT546.445.M37
Masai (African people)
  in
      Kenya: DT433.545.M33
      Tanzania: DT443.3.M37
Mascarene Islands: DT469.M39
Maseru (Lesotho): DT2683
Mashona (African people)
  in
      South Africa: DT1768.M38
      Zimbabwe: DT2913.M38
Mashonaland (Zimbabwe):
  DT3020.M37
Masire, Quett, 1980-    :
  DT2502
Massangano, Fall of (Mozambique):
  DT3374
Massaua (Eritrea): DT398.M3
Massawa (Eritrea); DT398.M3
Masvingo (Zimbabwe); DT3025.M37
Matabeleland (Zimbabwe):
  DT3020.M38
Matanzima, Kaiser: DT1949.M38
Material culture, Maori:
  DU423.I53
Matola (Mozambique): DT3415.M38
Matope (Zimbabwe); DT2940.M38
Matopo Hills (Zimbabwe):
  DT3020.M39
Mau Mau movement (Kenya):
  DT433.577
Maui (Hawaii): DU628.M3
Mauna Loa (Hawaii): DU629.M34
Maung (Australian people):
  DU125.M33

Mauretania (Morocco): DT318

Mauritania (French West Africa):
  DT554+

Mauritius: DT469.M4+

Mavura (Zimbabwe): DT2940.M39

Mawri (African people):
  DT547.45.M38

Mayombe (African people)
  in
      Zaire: DT650.M38

Mayotte: DT469.M497

Mbala (African people)
  in
      Zaire: DT650.M42

Mbalabala (Zimbabwe):
  DT3025.M43

Mbanane (Swaziland): DT2823

Mbandieru (African people)
  in
      Namibia: DT1558.M33

Mbandzeni: DT2780.M33

Mbane (Equatorial Guinea):
  DT620.9.E46

Mbanze (Angola): DT1465.M42

Mbere (African people)
  in
      Kenya: DT433.545.M34

Mbole (African people)
  in
      Zaire: DT650.M46

Mbum (African people):
  DT546.345.M38

Mbundu (African people)
  in
      Angola: DT1308.M38

Mbwila, Battle of, 1665:
  DT1378

McPherson Range (Australia):
  DU280.M22

Medical care (South African War):
  DT1918.M44

Medicine, Maori: DU423.M38

Medinet-Abu (Egypt): DT73.M3

Medinet Madi (Egypt): DT73.M35

Meetinghouses, Maori: DU423.M42

Megiddo, Battle of: DT87.2

Mejprat
  in
      Irian Jaya: DU744.35.M42

Mekhadma: DT346.M4

Melanesia: DU490

Melbourne (Australia): DU228

Memnon statue (Egypt): DT73.T32

Memphis (Egypt): DT73.M5

Mende
  in
      Sierra Leone: DT516.45.M45

Mendes (Egypt): DT73.M54

Menelik II (Ethiopia): DT387+

Menongue (Angola); DT1465.M46

Meroe (Sudan): DT159.9.M47

Meru (African people)
  in
      Kenya: DT433.545.M47

Metals (Egyptology): DT62.M5

Mfecane
  Mozambique: DT3366
  Natal: DT2238
  Orange Free State: DT2118
  South Africa: DT1841
  Southern Africa: DT1123
  Zambia: DT3087

Micronesia: DU500

Middle Congo: DT546.2+

Midway Islands (Hawaii):
  DU628.M5

Miklukha-Maklaĭ, Nikolaĭ
  Nikolaevich: DU746.M5

Milner, Alfred: DT1851.M55

Mina (African people):
  DT582.45.M55

Minyā Province (Egypt): DT73.M75

Miranda (Mozambique): DT3415.M33

Mirgissa (Sudan): DT159.9.M57

Mirrors (Egyptology): DT62.M58

Mlozi: DT3219.M56

Moba (African people)
  in
      Nigeria: DT515.45.M62

Mobuto Sese Seko, Regime of:
  DT658.25

Moçambique: DT3410.N36

Moçâmides (Angola)
  City: DT1465.N36
  Province: DT1450.N36

Moeris Lake (Egypt): DT73.M8

Moffat, Howard: DT2975.M64

Moffat, John: DT2963.M64

Moffat Treaty, 1888 (Zimbabwe):
  DT2955

Mohammed Ali, Khedive of Egypt:
  DT104

Mohammed Said, Viceroy of Egypt:
  DT105

Mohandas Gandhi, Civil
  disobedience campaigns by
  (Union of South Africa):
  DT1929

Mutu ya Kevela: DT1388.M88
Muzila: DT3364.M89
Muzorewa, Abel: DT2984.M89
Mvuma (Zimbabwe): DT3025.M88
Mwenezi (Zimbabwe): DT3025.M94
Mwila (African people)
  in
    Angola: DT1308.M85
Myene (African people)
  in
    Gabon: DT546.145.M93
Mzilikazi (Zimbabwe):
  DT2940.M95
Mzuzu (Malawi): DT3257.M98

## N

Naga-ed Dêr (Egypt): DT73.N2
Nalum
  in
    Irian Jaya: DU744.35.N32
Nama (African people)
  in
    Namibia: DT1558.N36
    South Africa: DT1768.N37
Nama War, 1904-1906: DT1620
Namaland (Namibia): DT1670.N36
Namaqualand (Little)
  South Africa: DT2400.N36
Namib Desert (Namibia): DT1670.N37
Namibe (Angola)
  City: DT1465.N36
  Province: DT1450.N36
Namibia: DT1501+
Nampula (Mozambique):DT3410.N36
Nande (African people)
  in
    Zaire: DT650.N34
Nandi (African people)
  in
    Kenya: DT433.545.N34
Naqādah (Egypt): DT73.N26
Nar (African people)
  in
    Chad: DT546.445.N35
Narangga (Australian people):
  DU125.N36
Narmouthis (Egypt): DT73.M35
Naron (African people)
  in
    South Africa: DT1768.N38
Narrinyeri (Australian people):
  DU125.N37

Nasser, Gamal Abdel, President
  United Arab Republic: DT107.83
Natal: DT2181+
Natal, Treks into: DT2242
National characteristics (South
  Africa): DT1755
National liberation and armed
  struggle by ANC, 1961-
  (South Africa): DT1953
National liberation movements
  (Southern Africa): DT1177
National liberation struggle,
  1964-1975 (Mozambique):
  DT3387
Naṭrūn Valley (Egypt): DT73.N28
Nauru: DU715
Navigators' Islands: DU810+
Ndebele (African people)
  in
    Transvaal under Mzilikazi:
      DT2340
    Zimbabwe: DT2913.N44
Ndebele invasions
  Zambia: DT3089
  Zimbabwe: DT2951
Ndebele War (Zimbabwe)
  1893: DT2966
  1896-1897: DT2968
Ndembu (African people)
  in
    Zambia: DT3058.N44
Ndendeuli (African people)
  in
    Tanzania: DT443.3.N43
Ndhir (Berber people)
  in
    Morocco: DT313.3.N4
Ndola (Zambia): DT3145.N46
Ndonga (African people)
  in
    Angola: DT1308.N46
    Namibia: DT1558.N46
Nefertete (Nefertiti), Consort
  of Amenhetep IV: DT87.45
Nefzaoua (Tunisia): DT268.N4
Nelson (New Zealand)
  Provincial District: DU430.N38
Netherlands New Guinea: DU744+
Neu Mecklenburg Island: DU553.N4
Neu Pommern Island: DU553.N35
New Britain Island: DU553.N35
New Caledonia: DU720
New Guinea: DU739+
New Hebrides: DU760

Nossi-Be (Madagascar):
  DT469.M37N67
Nova Freixo (Mozambique):
  DT3415.C83
Nova Lisboa (Angola): DT1465.H83
Novo Redondo (Angola): DT1465.N58
Ntomba (African people)
  in
    Zaire: DT650.N85
Ntombi, Queen Regent: DT2800.N86
Nuanetsi (Zimbabwe): DT3025.M94
Nuazira (Zimbabwe): DT3025.N83
Nuba (African people): DT155.2.N82
Nubia
  Egypt: DT159.6.N83
  Sudan: DT159.6.N83
Nuer (African people): DT155.2.N85
Nujoma, Sam: DT1641.N85
Nuku-hiva Island: DU701.N8
Nunggubuyu (Australian people):
  DU125.N94
Nunu (African people)
  in
    Congo: DT546.245.N86
Nupe (African people)
  in
    Nigeria: DT515.45.N86
Nursia (Australia): DU380.N4
Nyakyusa (African people)
  in
    Tanzania: DT443.3.N92
Nyamwezi (African people)
  in
    Tanzania: DT443.3.N93
Nyandoro, George: DT2979.N93
Nyaneka (African people)
  in
    Angola: DT1308.N93
Nyangatom (African people)
  in
    Ethiopia: DT380.4.N92
Nyanja (African people)
  in
    Malawi: DT3192.N83
    Mozambique: DT3328.N93
    Zambia: DT3058.N93
Nyasaland: DT3161+
Nyasaland Protectorate:
  DT3216+
Nyunga (Australian people):
  DU125.N97
Nzabi (African people)
  in
    Gabon: DT546.145.N93

Nzeto (Angola): DT1465.N94
Nzima (African people)
  in
    Ghana: DT510.43.N95
Nzinga, Queen of Matamba:
  DT1365.N95


O


Oahu (Hawaii): DU628.O3
Obasanjo administration
  (Nigeria): DT515.838
Obelisks (Egyptology): DT62.O2
Occupations (Gypsies): DX171
Oceania: DU1+
Ogori (African people)
  in
    Nigeria: DT515.45.O34
Okavango River and Swamp
  Botswana: DT2520.O53
  Namibia: DT1670.O63
Olivenca (Mozambique):
  DT3415.L87
Oltre Giuba (Italian colony):
  DT409.G58
Oran (Algeria)
  City: DT299.O7
  Province: DT298.O8
Orange Free State (South Africa):
  DT2075+
Orange Free State, Claims by
  (Lesotho): DT2630+
Orange River Colony, 1900-1910
  (Orange Free State): DT2139
Orange River sovereignty (Orange
  Free State): DT2122
Oranje Vrystaat (South Africa):
  DT2075+
Oromo (Ethiopia): DT390.G2
Ostraka (Egyptology): DT62.O88
Otago (New Zealand): DU430.O8
Ouled Nail: DT346.O8
Ouobe (African people)
  in
    Ivory Coast: DT545.45.O96
Ovambo (African people)
  in
    Angola: DT1308.O83
    Namibia: DT1558.O83
Owambo (Namibia): DT1670.O83
Oxyrhynchus (Egypt): DT73.O8

Population, Maori: DU423.P66
Port Elizabeth (South Africa):
   DT2405.P68
Port Said (Egypt): DT154.P7
Porto Amelia (Mozambique):
   DT3415.P45
Portraits (Maoris): DU422.8+
Portugália (Angola): DT1465.L83
Portuguese
   in
      Angola: DT1308.P68
      Gambia: DT509.45.P67
      Hawaii: DU624.7.P67
      Mozambique: DT3328.P68
      South Africa: DT1768.P67
Portuguese claims
   Equatorial Guinea: DT620.65+
   Malawi: DT3211+
   Namibia: DT1587+
   Zaire: DT654+
Portuguese colony and territory
   Guinea-Bissau: DT613.75+
   São Tomé and Principe: DT615.7
Portuguese consolidation (Angola):
   DT1385+
Portuguese expansion (Angola):
   DT1373+
Portuguese Guinea: DT613+
Portuguese penetration (Kenya):
   DT433.565+
Portuguese-speaking West Africa:
   DT591+
Potgieter, A.H.: DT2335.P68
Pottery (Egyptology): DT62.P72
Pretoria (South Africa): DT2403
Pretorius, Andries: DT2335.P84
Pretorius, M.W.: DT2350.P84
Prisoners and prisons (South
   African War): DT1918.P75
Private antiquities (Egyptology):
   DT66
Private collections (Egyptology):
   DT57.5
Ptolemais (Egypt): DT73.P8
Ptolemies, King of Egypt:
   DT92+
Public antiquities (Egyptology):
   DT65
Public opinion (South African
   War): DT1918.P83
Pukapuka Island (New Zealand):
   DU430.P8
Puluwat (Caroline Islands):
   DU568.P8

Pungua-Ndongo, Siege of, 1671:
   DT1380
Punt Kingdom (Eritrea): DT398.P8
Pushtuns
   in
      Australia: DU122.P87
Pygmies: DT16.P8
   in
      Cameroon: DT571.P93
      French West Africa:
         DT530.5.P94
      Zaire: DT650.P94
Pyramids (Egyptology): DT63+

**Q**

Qacha's Nek (Lesotho):
   DT2686.Q33
Qasr al-Sagha Region (Egypt):
   DT73.Q35
Qasr Qarun (Egypt): DT73.D56
Qift (Egypt): DT73.Q54
Quarries (Egyptology): DT62.Q8
Que Que (Zimbabwe): DT3025.K84
Queensland (Australia): DU250+
el-Qurna (Egypt): DT73.Q75
Qurnat Murā'i Hill (Egypt):
   DT73.Q76
Qusayr al-Qadīm (Egypt):
   DT73.Q77
Quthing (Lesotho): DT2686.Q87
QwaQwa (South Africa): DT2400.Q83

**R**

Race relations
   Angola: DT1306
   Botswana: DT2456
   Cape Province: DT2032
   Malawi: DT3190
   Mozambique: DT3326
   Namibia: DT1555
   Natal: DT2222
   Orange Free State: DT2102
   South Africa: DT1756
   Southern Africa: DT1056
   Transvaal: DT2322
   Zambia: DT3056
   Zimbabwe: DT2912
Radama, King of Madagascar
   I: DT469.M323
   II: DT469.M326

Rahanweyn
  in
      Somalia: DT402.4.R35
Rameses, King of Egypt
  II: DT88
  III: DT88.8
Ramesseum (Egypt); DT73.T33
Ranavalona (Ranavalo), Queen of
    Madagascar
  I: DT469.M324
  II: DT469.M33
  III: DT469.M335
Rand Gold rush begins, 1886
    (South Africa): DT1888
Rand Revolt, 1922 (Union of
    South Africa): DT1935
Rangi (African people)
  in
      Tanzania: DT443.3.R35
Raqqada (Tunisia): DT269.R35
Ras Taffari (Tafari)
    Makonnen: DT387.6
Rashāyidah (Arab people)
  in
      Sudan: DT155.2.R37
Rasoherina, Queen of Madagascar:
    DT469.M328
Rehoboth (Namibia): DT1685.R46
Rehoboth Basters
  in
      Namibia: DT1558.R45
      South Africa: DT1768.R45
Rehoboth Basters' Rebellion, 1925:
    DT1632
Rehoboth Basters' settlement,
    1868: DT1597
Rehoboth Basters Uprising, 1915:
    DT1622
Religion (Gypsies): DX151
Religion, Maori: BL2615
Religious antiquities (Egyptology):
    DT68+
Rendile (African people)
  in
      Kenya: DT433.545.R45
Republic of Liberia: DT634+
Republic of South Africa: DT1945+
Retief, Piet: DT2235.R48
    Death of: DT2245+
Réunion: DT469.R3+
Revolution
    Angola, 1961-1975: DT1398+
    Equatorial Guinea, 1979:
      DT620.8+

Revolution - Continued
    Guinea-Bissau, 1963-1974:
      DT613.78
    Hawaiian Islands, 1893-1898:
      DU627.19+
Rhodes, Cecil John: DT1851.R56
Rif (Berber people)
  in
      Morocco: DT313.3.R53
Rif Mountains (Morocco): DT328.R5
Rio de Oro: DT346.S7
Rites and ceremonies, Maori:
    DU423.R55
Rivonia Trial, 1964: DT1955
Rizeiqāt (Egypt): DT73.R5
Roberto, Holden: DT1417.R63
Roberts, Joseph Jenkins:
    DT633.3.R6
Rock Temple of el-Derr (Egypt):
    DT73.D492
Rodrigues Island: DT469.M492
Rogoro (African people)
  in
      Tanzania: DT443.3.R64
Rolong (African people)
  in
      Botswana: DT2458.R75
      South Africa: DT1768.R65
Roman period (North Africa):
    DT170
Roman rule (Egypt): DT93+
Rorke's Drift, Battle of:
    DT1879.R68
Rotorua (New Zealand): DU430.R6
Rottnest Island (Australia):
    DU380.R68
Rozwi Empire, ca. 1700-1834:
    DT2947
Rozwi Kingdoms: DT1117
Ruanda-Urundi: DT450+
Rudd Concession, 1888 (Zimbabwe):
    DT2957
Rufa'a al-Hoi (African people):
    DT155.2.R83
Rukuba (African people)
  in
      Nigeria: DT515.45.R84
Rulers (Sudan): DT155.42
Rundi: DT450.65.R86
Russel, George: DU222.R8
Russians
  in
      Australia: DU122.R8
      Hawaii: DU624.7.R87

Shaba (Zaire): DT665.K3
Shaba Invasions, 1977-1978:
  DT658.25
Shabani (Zimbabwe): DT3025.Z95
Shaikia (Arab people): DT155.2.S45
Shambala (African people)
  in
     Tanzania: DT443.3.S45
Shangaan, War with (Mozambique):
  DT3381
Shangana: DT3364.S5
Sharpe, Alfred: DT3219.S53
Sharpeville Massacre, 1960 (Union
  of South Africa): DT1941
Sharpeville Massacre Anniversary,
  1985 (Republic of South Africa):
  DT1965
Shepstone, Theophilus: DT2254.S54
Shilluks (African people):
  DT155.2.S46
Ships (Egyptology): DT62.S55
Shire River and Valley (Malawi):
  DT3252.S55
Shisilweni (Swaziland): DT2820.S55
Shona Uprising, 1896 (Zimbabwe):
  DT2970
Shurugwe (Zimbabwe): DT3025.S58
Sidamas
  in
    Ethiopia: DT380.4.S5
Sierra Leone: DT516+
Silva Porto (Angola): DT1465.K85
Silva Porto, Francisco da:
  DT1376.S56
Sinai Peninsula: DS110.5
Sipolilo (Zimbabwe): DT3025.G87
Sipopa: DT3081.S56
Sisala (African people)
  in
    Ghana: DT510.43.S57
Sisulu, Walter: DT1949.S58
Siteki (Swaziland): DT2825.S58
Sithole, Ndabaningi: DT2984.S58
Siwa Oasis (Egypt): DT154.S5
Skeleton Coast (Namibia):
  DT1670.S64
Slaghter's Nek incident, 1815
  (South Africa): DT1839
Smith, Ian: DT2984.S65
Smuts, Jan Christiaan: DT1927.S68
Sobhuza II: DT2802
Social conditions, Maori: DU423.S6
Social life and customs, Maori:
  DU423.S63

Society Islands: DU870
Sofala (Mozambique): DT3410.S65
Sofala, Attack of (Mozambique):
  DT3370
Solomon Islands: DU850
Somali-Ethiopian Conflict,
  1977-   : DT387.952
Somalia: DT401+
Somaliland: DT401+
Somalis
  in
    Ethiopia: DT380.4.S65
    foreign countries (General):
      DT402.45
Somba (African people)
  in
    Benin: DT541.45.S65
Songe (African people)
  in
    Zaire: DT650.S55
Songhai (African people)
  in
    French West Africa:
      DT530.5.S65
    Niger: DT547.45.S65
Songhai empire: DT532.27
Soninke (African people)
  in
    Senegal: DT549.45.S66
Sorbs
  in
    Australia: DU122.S67
Sosso (African people)
  in
    Angola: DT1308.S68
Sotho (African people)
  in
    Botswana: DT2458.S78
    South Africa: DT1768.S68
The Sotho, War against (Orange
  Free State)
  1858: DT2129
  1865-1866: DT2133
Soudanese Republic: DT551+
South Africa: DT1701+
South African administration
  (Namibia): DT1638+
South African incursions,
  1978-   (Angola): DT1436
South African invasions,
  1975-1976 (Angola): DT1430
South African Mandate: DT1625+
South African Mandate, 1966,
  Cancellation of: DT1643

250

South African Native National
  Congress, 1912, Founding of:
  DT1931
South African raid on Maseru,
  1982: DT2658
South African Republic: DT2291+
South African War, 1899-1902:
  DT1890+
South Africans
  in
    foreign countries (General):
      DT1770
South Seas: DU1+
South-West Africa: DT1501+
Southern Africa: DT1001+
Southern Region (Sudan):
  DT159.6.S73
Southern Rhodesia: DT2871+
Southern Sudan question:
  DT157.67
Southern Territories (Algeria):
  DT298.S6
Southern Zones (Spanish Morocco):
  DT330
Southland (New Zealand): DU430.S6
Soweto (South Africa): DT2405.S68
Soweto uprising, 1976: DT1959
Soweto uprising anniversary, 1986:
  DT1969
Spaniards
  in
    Algeria: DT283.6.S62
    Australia: DU122.S73
Spanish Guinea: DT620+
Spanish Morocco: DT330
Spanish Sahara: DT346.S7
Spanish West Africa: DT619+
Sparterie (Egyptology): DT62.S67
Sphinxes (Egyptology): DT62.S7
Spoons (Egyptology): DT62.S73
St. Brandon Island: DT469.M495
St. Helena Islands: DT671.S2
Stanleyville (Zaire): DT665.K55
State of emergency, 1985-
  (Republic of South Africa):
  1967
Statesmen (Sudan): DT155.46
Stel, Simon van der: DT1817.S84
Steles (Egyptology): DT62.S8
Stellaland and Goshen, 1882-1884:
  DT2366
Stewart Island (New Zealand):
  DU430.S7
Steyn, M.T.: DT2127.S84

Stormberg, Battle of, 1899:
  DT1908.S87
Strzelecki, Sir Paul Edmund de:
  DU172.S77
Suba (African people)
  in
    Kenya: DT433.545.S83
Sudan: DT154.1+
Sudanese
  in
    Uganda: DT433.245.S92
Suez (Isthmus and Canal)
  Egypt: DT154.S9
Suk (African people)
  in
    Kenya: DT433.545.S85
Sukarno, Mount: DU747.S8
Suki
  in
    Tanzania: DT443.3.S84
Superstition (Gypsies): DX151
Suvaroff Island: DU860
Suvarrow Islands: DU860
Suwaroff Islands: DU860
Swahili-speaking peoples
  in
    Eastern Africa: DT365.45.S93
Swakop River and Valley (Namibia):
  DT1650.S83
Swakopmund (Namibia): DT1685.S83
Swaziland: DT2701+
Swedes
  in
    Australia: DU122.S94
    Ethiopia: DT380.4.S94
Swellendam Rebellion, 1795:
  DT1835
Swinburne, George: DU222.S8
Swiss
  in
    Australia: DU122.S95
Sydney (Australia): DU178
Syrians
  in
    Egypt: DT72.S9

**T**

Tabwa (African people):
  DT443.3.T32
Taha Husayn: DT107.2.T3
Tahiti Islands: DU870
Ṭaḥrīr Province (Egypt): DT137.T3

Toilet articles (Egyptology):
DT62.T5
Toivo ja Toivo, Andimba:
DT1641.T75
Tokelau Islands: DU910
Tolbert, William R.: DT636.4.T63
Tolemaide (Libya): DT239.T6
Tombs (Egyptology): DT62.T6
Tonga Islands: DU880
Tongaland (South Africa):
DT2400.T66
Tongaland, Incorporation of
(Natal): DT2261
Tools (Egyptology): DT62.T65
Torres Strait (Australia):
DU280.T7
Torres Strait Islanders
(Australian people): DU125.T67
Toucouleur empire: DT532.3
Toucouleurs (African people)
in
Senegal: DT549.45.T68
Touggourt (Algeria): DT299.T7
Toure, Ahmed Sekou: DT543.82.T68
Trades (Gypsies): DX171
Transitional government
Namibia: DT1648
Zimbabwe: DT2994
Transkei (South Africa):
DT2400.T83
Transkei Revolt, 1880: DT1884
Transorangia: DT2112+
Transorangia, Treks into:
DT2120
Transvaal: DT2291+
Transvaal, Treks into: DT2342
Transvaal rule, 1894-1902
(Swaziland): DT2793
Treaty of Aliwal North and cession
of Sotho lands, 1869 (Orange
Free State): DT2135
Trigo de Morais (Mozambique):
DT3415.C58
Tripoli (Libya): DT211+
City: DT239.T7
Tripolitania: DT238.T8
Tristan da Cunha Islands:
DT671.T8
Trobriand Islands: DU885
Truk Islands: DU568.T7
Tsana Lake (Ethiopia):
DT390.T8
Tsholotsho (Zimbabwe):
DT3025.T85

Tswana (African people)
in
Botswana: DT2458.T89
South Africa: DT1768.T89
Zimbabwe: DT2913.T78
Tuamotu Islands: DU890
Tuaregs
in
Algeria: DT283.6.T83
Niger: DT547.45.T83
Sahara: DT346.T7
Tubman, William V.S.: DT636.T8
Tubuai Islands: DU900
Tuggurt (Algeria): DT299.T7
Tumbuka (African people)
in
Malawi: DT3192.T85
Tunāt al-Jabal Site (Egypt):
DT73.T85
Tunis (Tunisia): DT269.T8
Tunisia (Tunis): DT241+
Turco-Italian War, 1911-1912:
DT234
Turkana (African people)
in
Kenya: DT433.545.T87
Turkish rule (Egypt): DT97+
Turks
in
Libya: DT223.2.T85
Turnhalle conference, 1975-     :
DT1647
Tusia (African people)
in
Burkina Faso: DT555.45.T87
Tutenkhamun, King of Egypt:
DT87.5
Tuvalu: DU590
Twat: DT346.T8


U


Uap (Caroline Islands): DU568.Y3
Ubangi-Shari: DT546.3+
Ubium (African people)
in
Nigeria: DT515.45.U24
Uduk (African people):
DT155.2.U38
Uganda: DT433.2+
Uganda-Tanzania War, 1978-1979:
DT433.283

Yalunka (African people)
  in
    Sierra Leone: DT516.45.Y34
Yamba, Dauti: DT3106.Y35
Yangura (Australian people):
  DU125.Y35
Yanzi (Bantu people)
  in
    Zaire: DT650.Y3
Yao
  in
    Malawi: DT3192.Y36
    Mozambique: DT3328.Y36
Yap (Caroline Islands):
  DU568.Y3
Yatenga (Kingdom): DT532.33
Yei
  in
    Irian Jaya: DU744.35.Y44
Yombe (African people)
  in
    Zambia: DT3058.Y66
Yorubas (African people)
  in
    Nigeria: DT515.45.Y67
    West Africa: DT474.6.Y67
Youth, Maori: DU423.C5
Yugoslavs
  in
    Australia: DU122.Y8
    New Zealand: DU424.5.Y84


**Z**

Zaire: DT641+
Zaire Province (Angola): DT1450.Z35

Zambezi Rebellion, 1917
  (Mozambique): DT3385
Zambezi River and Valley (Southern
  Africa): DT1190.Z36
Zambia: DT3031+
Zambia (Mozambique): DT3410.Z36
Zanzibar: DT449.Z2+
Zarma (African people)
  in
    Niger: DT547.45.Z37
Zauditu, Waizeru, Empress of
  Ethiopia: DT387.6
Zela (African people): DT650.Z44
Zezuru (African people)
  in
    Zimbabwe: DT2913.Z49
Zimbabwe: DT2871+
Zomba (Malawi): DT3257.Z66
Zomba Plateau (Malawi):
  DT3252.Z65
Zulu (African people)
  in
    South Africa: DT1768.Z95
Zulu conquest of Lourenco
  Marques, 1833: DT3368
Zulu Empire: DT1119
Zulu-Indian riots, 1949 (Natal):
  DT2275
Zulu War, 1879: DT1875+
Zululand (South Africa):
  DT2400.Z85
Zululand, Incorporation of
  (Natal): DT2261
Zuwaya
  in
    Libya: DT223.2.Z87
Zvishavane (Zimbabwe): DT3025.Z95

✩U.S. G.P.O. 1989-237-190